Stop Bullying Yourself

STOP
BULLYING
YOURSELF!

Identify Your Inner Bully,
Get Out of Your Own Way
and Enjoy Greater Health, Wealth,
Happiness and Success.

Anna Marie Frank

NEW YORK

LONDON • NASHVILLE • MELBOURNE • VANCOUVER

STOP BULLYING YOURSELF

Identify Your Inner Bully, Get Out of Your Own Way and Enjoy Greater Health, Wealth, Happiness and Success

Published in New York, New York, by Morgan James Publishing. Morgan James is a trademark of Morgan James, LLC. www.MorganJamesPublishing.com

The Morgan James Speakers Group can bring authors to your live event. For more information or to book an event visit The Morgan James Speakers Group at www.TheMorganJamesSpeakersGroup.com.

ISBN 9781683507918 paperback
ISBN 9781683507925 eBook
Library of Congress Control Number: 2017915638

Cover Design by:
Rachel Lopez
www.r2cdesign.com

Interior Design by:
Chris Treccani
www.3dogcreative.net

In an effort to support local communities, raise awareness and funds, Morgan James Publishing donates a percentage of all book sales for the life of each book to Habitat for Humanity Peninsula and Greater Williamsburg.

Get involved today! Visit
www.MorganJamesBuilds.com

Table of Contents

Disclaimer: This book should not be viewed as medical or psychiatric intervention; however, for the vast majority of readers, if you are receptive, this book will give you the opportunity to learn, grow and discover what true happiness and inner peace feel like.

Dedication

This book is dedicated to my children. May you have lasting inner peace from a young age and the determination to strive towards greatness in all aspects of your life. To my husband, thank you for your love and support. To all my family, thank you for everything! I know I've been able to write this book because of all of the people that have come into and out of my life and I am thankful for those people. To my best friend, Caroline Hatty, for always being positive and showing me what a true friend is. To all the mentors in my life, thank you for your time and guidance. Most importantly, I thank God for having allowed all the "negative" things into my life as lessons to learn from. God has given each of us a powerful mind along with the wonderful gift of choice and I am very thankful for that. This book is also dedicated to anyone who has ever struggled to find inner peace, true happiness, and satisfaction in life.

A special thank you to my editor, Guitta Karubian, your guidance during this process was life changing!

A very special thank you to Haleigh Vanderstelt for designing the book cover and helping create the images provided throughout the book. You can contact Haleigh for design work at: www.HaleighVanderstelt.com

Introduction

"The only person you are destined to become
is the person you decide to be."
–RALPH WALDO EMERSON

Life Can Be an Awkward Dance

I envision my life journey as an awkward dance. I have taken steps forward and many steps back. My life-dance has never been perfect and many days my past dance felt awkward. Some days I felt like I was stumbling. In my past, my days of gracelessness left me wishing for some help in choreographing my life. I found myself wishing for specific steps to take, for certain specific things to happen, as if my wishes would just fall out of the sky and into my life. I looked outward for a way to make my life-dance more divine, more satisfying, when I should have been looking inward at myself.

I learned you can't just wish for things, you must reprogram yourself to take action and be open to the unknown, and accept the unfulfilled wishes. In retrospect, I'm thankful God didn't give me what I'd wished for because it has been the awkward missteps in my life's journey that have provided me the greatest lessons that I now get to share with you. We can learn so very much from our imperfections and challenges in life, as long as we take control of our life and not allow our inner bully to flourish.

> *"You've gotta dance like there's nobody watching, Love like you'll never be hurt, Sing like there's nobody listening, and live like it's heaven on earth."*
> –WILLIAM W. PURKEY

The surprises in life, as in your dance, can be both exciting and energizing. You need to capture these moments and really dance like no one is watching. On the flip side, don't try to dance too carefully, too perfectly or try to anticipate your every move. The fearful voice of your inner bully will cause you to do this. If you move too carefully, you will not grow, and when you try to anticipate every little future move you begin to hope certain things will come to pass. You try to anticipate everything and that anticipation distracts you from the beauty of spontaneity. When you are anticipating any one thing, you may miss the opportunity to dance your true destiny. Don't wish for comfort and ease in life; instead, develop more skills and be more open to growth. Most importantly, be careful what you wish for. Remember, develop yourself, build skills and challenge yourself. Don't get caught up in the wishing game, looking outward for perfection, or your inner bully will control your life.

I will help you uncover the ultimate key to a successful life by becoming able to recognize your inner bully when it tries to cut into your life-dance and take over. You can prevent this from happening. In your moments of both weakness and strength, the inner bully camouflages itself. It is up to you to recognize these moments of "bully madness."

Your inner bully is always waiting. You're especially vulnerable to it when you have self-doubt, and when you wish, pray, or hope for something that is not meant to be. You will ask why something did or didn't happen. You get so caught up with what is not happening that you miss what is happening. You may blame God, wondering why He didn't answer your prayers. You may blame yourself, thinking, *"What's wrong with me, why didn't this happen?"*

What we may want at a specific time may not be meant to be; it may never be meant to be. Often, it's a blessing that some of these wishes, prayers, hopes, don't come to fruition. When you are faced with such challenging times and when something you want is not there for you, be thankful for the things that are. Be thankful for the moments you do have. You must always focus on the good, positive stuff that is in your life.

I remember being in a relationship and praying that we would marry. I believed that if we just lived closer the man I cared for would ask me to marry him; so, I prayed that the distance between us would lessen and we would be closer—a closer apartment or a closer job. I was praying to dance with a partner who was not good for me. While I was praying that we would marry, he cheated on me. It made me feel so insignificant! I felt like something was wrong with me! I beat myself up because I assumed he cheated on me because I wasn't good enough. My inner bully gleefully came out to tell me just how small I was. I lost sight of a lot of good things that were happening in my life at that time, because I was too focused on what I didn't have.

Of course, I now know that I could have handled the situation differently. When he was short with me on the phone and then stopped calling, my gut knew something was wrong; my inner bully told me that it was me. The best way for me to have handled it would be to pray for wisdom, smarter dance steps and a better dance partner. Focusing on the positive things in my life then would have given me perspective. I should have listened to my gut. Deep down we all know what is best for us, but our inner bully can block our clarity and confuse us. We need to remove negative self-talk, so we can clearly see what we truly need and how much we already have—especially when things are tough.

Can you imagine how ugly my life's dance would have been if I had married a cheater? I could have been years into a marriage, maybe with children, and then found myself in the mess of a divorce. You know the saying, "Be careful what you wish for." Well, be careful whom you dance with, too!

Are you ready to stand up to your inner bully, accept your past, own it and be thankful for every bit of it? Are you ready to reprogram your mind and stop playing the wishing game? My hope for you is by the time you are done with this book you will be directing your life-dance in the right direction, without worry or lack of confidence while embracing all that you have been through. I want to join you in your life-dance, for a short period of time, just long enough to help you approach life in a *wholistic* new mindful, bully-free way.

"Live your truth. Express your love. Share your enthusiasm. Take action towards your dreams. Walk your talk. Dance and sing to your music. Embrace your blessings. Make today worth remembering."
–STEVE MARABOLI

I analogize life as a dance with each event a step in your performance, a step in your life. You are always moving. You may move forwards or backwards in life. You may even feel like you are twirling around or even leaping towards or away from something. Some people seem to move more gracefully in life, while others seem to have two left feet. Some may be reluctant to dance freely while others love the dance of life no matter what. We all are moving through life, dancing to our different beats. Choose to be a happy dancer, move to the music of your life in your own unique way and do not allow your inner bully to lead your life-dance.

I want you to allow yourself to open up, learn a new way to dance in life without your inner bully's influence. To do this you need to learn from your past and embrace it—the good, the bad, and the ugly. You must accept all of it and own it. Do not allow yourself to use your past against you. Use your past to enhance you (I will teach you how to do this). You need to take responsibility for all your past actions and for your choices. Once you take ownership of your past, you can reprogram yourself to become unstoppable and be a happy, successful individual who enjoys *your* life-dance no matter what. Embrace all your missteps in your life-dance and you will grow from your mistakes. Remember, no two dances or dancers are the same, a truth which gives your unique performance such beauty.

*"The one thing you have that no one else has is you. Your voice,
your mind, your story, your vision. So, write and draw and build and
play and dance and live only as you can."*
−NEIL GAIMAN

Congrats for choosing to pick up this book and taking time for you. Here you will find information that will both inspire you to live the life you dream of and also provide you with the tools you need to have that life. You will learn to give yourself a break and not be so hard on yourself, all while taking action to move you closer to your goals and dreams. Your personal thoughts and experiences will also prove to be all-important as your new life evolves. For that reason, the material here is presented in an interactive format, allowing you to see how it affects *you* and *your* unique life experience.

This book consists of lessons I've learned as the result of personal experiences over many years and I will show you how you can draw on your own past, as lessons learned, to enhance your present and your future. You will find that a number of the concepts I present here overlap. That is because it is the practiced interconnection, which is the essence of what I call a *wholistic* life. I spell *wholistic* with a *"W"* because you need to be a *whole* person. Holistic medicine treats the *whole* person. I want you to treat every aspect of your life with mindfulness. When you join the *whole* approach with the holistic approach to life, the inner bully cannot survive the *wholistic* environment and that is what this book will teach you—that the negative, destructive voice inside your mind that holds you back in life and puts a ceiling on the level of success you experience will not survive. You will no longer let this voice suppresses your happiness or feed your fears, the inner bull, will not be successful in controlling your life once you are done with this book. I've also added some great quotes throughout the book that are energizing and refreshing as well as inspirational, so please take some time to pause and reflect on them. On your journey to becoming a more happy-whole-you connect with the Happy-Whole-You community by visiting our social media sites and stay connected on **www.HappyWholeYou.com**. Join the challenges, share your results, and sign-up for the Happy-Whole-You free newsletter.

> *"You can't go back and make a new start, but you can start right now and make a brand-new ending."*
> –JAMES R. SHERMAN

A Word about Answering Questions

There will be many questions you'll be asking yourself in the pages ahead. You'll be writing some detailed (private) information about yourself and I encourage you to really think and include every possible detail you can in each section; one-word answers are frowned upon and there are no wrong answers. Your inner bully will be watching and discouraging you from writing down full and honest answers, so be careful!

No matter what your age, remember that as you work through this book, you will gain a better understanding of yourself by doing the exercises. You may feel challenged and that's a good thing. Those of you with a lot of life experience may have a hard time because your inner bully has been programming your mind for a longer time. Those of you with less life experience may feel challenged because you have a limited amount of personal experience to draw from. Whatever the case, don't get frustrated! Just take time to get laser focused on the questions and answer each of them to the best of your ability. You'll find your potential for growth lies within your challenges.

Once you finish this book and you start implementing changes brought on by what you've learned, return to the questions and approach them with fresh answers. Then compare your answers, so you can see what areas you're showing growth in and what areas still need your attention.

If you stay true to yourself and the process of completing this book, you will learn that every aspect of your life is interconnected and that you are always in control of your growth, happiness, and success. Your answers will demonstrate this.

I assume those of you reading this book are twelve years old or older. If you're a teenager, be open to looking at the big picture of your life and future. I remember that when I was a teen, I couldn't imagine what it would be like to be 25 years old, let alone 35 or 45; that sounded so old to me! Let me tell you, at 30, life is just beginning.

I want you to be mindful that your emotional maturity and emotional well-being also impact how you answer the questions posed. You need to be reflective and ask yourself, "Why do I feel this way?" "Why did I answer this question this way?" Keep digging deeper and question your answers. The goal is for you to identify and expose your inner bully when it cuts in and tries to bring you down.

Remember: *Your inner bully wants you to fail!* Yes, even here, even now. So, this will be a test of your ability to overcome your internal bully. It is a measure of how much you truly want to succeed.

> *"The most common way people give up their power is by thinking they don't have any."*
> –ALICE WALKER

The Inner Bully

What is the Inner Bully?

Do you know anyone who is a bully? Hopefully you don't, but what about someone who bullies themselves? When you think about it, we all do it. We replay negative self-talk. We question our own abilities. We limit our potential. Why the heck do we do this? We all crave happiness and have a desire to live a fulfilling life; yet, we ourselves jump in the way of this. How can that be? We are, after all, the ones that want happiness and success—right? Instead of being boundless and wild, we set limits on our goals and dreams. We do this in all areas of our lives. This is an oxymoron if you ask me—I want happiness and success, but not too much, and not if I have to work too hard, because what will happen if I fail?

I need to ask you; do you ever feel you're just coming up a little short? Or maybe you feel stuck and wonder why you're still struggling despite doing all the right things? Why haven't you gotten the promotion you've been working towards? Why do your relationships always seem problematic? Why does life just seem so hard? Have you ever wanted to learn something new like a language, or skill, but don't? Have you ever wanted to exercise more and eat better, but have done neither? Have you ever wanted to volunteer more, or keep your house cleaner, or take a trip, but haven't? Why? Your life would be enriched and you would be a healthier and happier person, so why haven't you done any of those multitudes of things or the many you could probably think of? The answer is that your inner bully is leading your life's dance. Yes, you, the very person reading this! *You* are the biggest bully of all. Now before you challenge yourself to a fight on the playground, let me explain. You, and only you, are allowing your inner bully to fill your head with doubt and negative self-talk. Are you getting this? The good news is that it isn't your circumstances or those of someone else holding you back in life. You are holding yourself back from dancing freely. And the great news is that I am here to help you free yourself from your bully moments.

You have an inner voice, a voice that tells you how great you are. But all too often, tells you that you are anything *but* great. It tells you be *"practical,"* and *"don't dream too big."* It says, *"You're not good enough,"* and, *"You deserve just what you have and nothing more."* It can try to convince you that you are "somehow less" than those around you.

You can try to not pay attention to this negative voice, but if it's not dealt with, it will eventually be too loud to ignore and can destroy your dreams, aspirations, relationships—in short, damage the quality of your life. It can stomp on your spirit and hold you down. This is the voice of *your* inner bully. The difference between a happy, successful person and everyone else is that the successful person has learned how to win the battle with this inner voice, so they can dance freely (read the introduction for more on the dance of life).

You can be smart, talented, and awesome, but your inner bully can convince you that you are average, stupid, untalented, and even a loser. If you're a recent grad, your inner bully can make your feel as if you have no skills and don't belong anywhere. It's the inner bully that will make a new mom feel guilty because she's chosen to work or make her feel unsuccessful if she's chosen to stay home with her new baby. The inner bully encourages you to stay at a boring job because you fear you'll never find anything better, you're too old to change jobs, or you're too invested there to start your own business. The inner bully uses the fear of failure to play you like a puppet. The inner bully tries to overpower your spirit, slow you down, and ultimately prevent you from pursuing your passions and desires.

Your inner bully is sneaky; you may deny you even have one. *News flash!* You have an inner bully. I have an inner bully. Everyone does! Unfortunately, most people pass up the opportunity to deal with this fact. Those of you that grab ahold of it and confront it by using the strategies given in this book will experience a more abundant, *whole* life. The longer you fail to address this madness in your mind, the less productive you will be, the more negative your outlook will become, and the less money you will make. You *must* address your inner bully in order to grow. You must suffocate the destructive words you say to yourself so you succeed!

The answers are in the pages ahead. As you'll learn, it's an easy thing to do, though it has many parts.

I know all about the inner bully. I had allowed my inner bully to control my happiness and success for years before I learned how to dominate it. In writing this book, it is my hope that you can take my experiences and utilize what I've learned to help yourself or someone you love. A great leader once asked me, "Why the heck would you wait and try to figure it all out on your own when you can pick up a book, and within a few hours learn what he or she took years to learn?" Great point, right? It has taken me many years to learn these truths, years filled with some tough lessons, and it is with great honor and tremendous excitement that I'm now sharing with you the tools and action steps that will help you become a more *happy-whole-you*.

"You have within you, right now, everything you need to deal with whatever the world can throw at you."
–BRIAN TRACY

Worksheet #1—Trash Can

I have prepared a variety of worksheets that you'll see throughout this book to aid you in becoming a more Happy-Whole-You. This first worksheet is your Happy-Whole-You Trash Can. Before venturing on, take a moment and visualize yourself throwing away all your negative inner bully energy. You have the opportunity to take every negative thing in your life and throw it in the trash. Think of everything you no longer want or things you want to change, now write it down on the shapes provided in the trashcan. Once you are finished, look at what you no longer want and then rip this page out and throw it away. Yes, throw it away! From now on, if you find yourself surrounded or doing something you wrote on this sheet, I want you to visualize yourself throwing it away. If you wrote down "Stop eating ice cream late at night," when you get the craving to grab that spoon and bowl I want you to visualize yourself throwing that habit away. If you spend a lot of time playing games on your tablet or cell phone, you'll visualize deleting those games. This will be a great reminder that your habit is trash and it is not helping you move towards your goals. By writing down all the negative things you want to change or get rid of you are helping yourself throw them away forever. You can print a larger copy from my HappyWholeYou.com website.

1. Write down any negative thing you do not want in your life on a shape
2. Also, write down anything you want to change on a shape
3. Take a moment and reread each item
4. Tear out this page or print a copy from the website
5. Wad up this trash can
6. Throw it in the trash
7. Every time you think of one of these "trash can" items, visualize the moment you threw it away.

This WORKS!

TRASH CAN

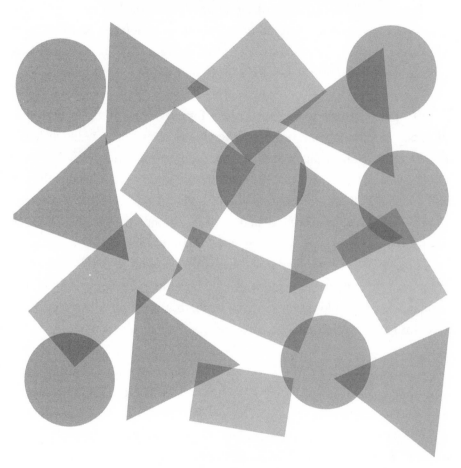

www.HappyWholeYou.com

My Life Rules

To succeed in most things, you have to know the rules that govern it, and life is no different. Some of the things I've learned in my years were not always easy lessons. I've narrowed my most important life rules down to these; you may have heard some of them before. I hope so. They are good rules to live by if your goal is to be a happy-healthy-successful person.

#1: The world is not fair, so move forward! You were all born into different families, grew up in different circumstances with different opportunities and you have different genetics and abilities. It is not your circumstances, but rather, what you do with your circumstances and with your abilities that will create your opportunities and impact your life positively. Count your blessings every day and *create* your opportunities. Don't throw a fit; accept that you have what you have. You must take what you see as the "unfairness of life," embrace it and use it to fuel your desires. After all, if life were "fair" and we all had the same things, the same opportunities, and similar lives, it would diminish much of the beauty in our diversity. Don't wish for fairness. *Work towards progress. Your life is up to you!*

#2: Happiness is a choice! You have a choice every single morning when you wake up. This is when your happy day starts. You can grumble, hit the alarm clock, roll over and stay in bed, or you can swing your feet around, place them firmly on the floor, stand up, stretch, and smile. The choice is an easy one to make: do you get up or stay in bed?

Even when you're feeling down, the most important thing you can do is remind yourself of all that is good in your life. You can either choose to see the positive and be excited about another day filled with blessings allowing you to move towards your goals or you can dwell on the negative, close your eyes, whine and refuse to participate in life. Choose happiness! Choose a positive attitude and you'll be glad you did. *Choose to stand up and smile!*

#3: Start saving and find joy in what you do! Money is easy to make, but harder to keep! The key to financial success is not, as you might think, winning the lottery or getting a high-paying job. The first key to amassing wealth is to love how you earn money. Then begin saving. If you haven't already begun saving money, start now. You can do that by resolving that you will no longer waste money on expensive, unnecessary things like lattes, monthly subscriptions that you don't use or that don't help you grow, and other expenses that do not add value to your life. Find the little ways your money slips away, and end those leaks now. Start putting that money to good use for your future.

You're not sure why you have no money to save? You can't figure out where it all went? The only way you can know how you're spending your money is to write down every single thing you spend it on for at least a full week. You may be shocked at the spending patterns you find. Another way to save money is to save your discounts. People confuse "saving" with "discounting." Have you ever told a friend how much money you "saved" on a shopping trip? You go to the store and find a great deal on a sweater. It cost you $30 versus $50. Did you save $20? If you told me that you did, I would ask, "Did you put the money you saved into a savings account?" You know the answer to that: *Nope!* You can only say you saved money if you took that $20 and put it in the bank or in a retirement account. I challenge you to write down all the money you spend for a week and keep more of your money by investing your discounts.

You don't love what you're doing? Why? What *are* you passionate about? Can you bring that passion to your work? Find ways to enjoy your work and enhance your work environment. Most of you work forty hours a week. Shouldn't you enjoy that time? If you just can't find anyway to enjoy what you do by the time you finish this book, maybe it is time to start looking somewhere else for a happier way to create income. *Bring passion into your work and start to save!*

#4: You are surrounded by what you want, and you are what you surround yourself with! Some people call this the "law of attraction," but I call it the "law of choice." You can choose who and what you surround yourself with. Do you choose to be around positive, productive people or do you choose to be around complainers? Do you make choices at the market that will fill your fruit bowl and vegetable drawer, so that when you open your fridge you will have colorful, healthy choices to eat or do you buy unhealthy food? Do the colors of your walls at home close in on you and depress you, or do you choose to paint your walls with clean, happy colors? Yes, I just suggested that you change the colors in your home to improve your mood to bring you success. I have done this and can tell you that it works! Every single thing you surround yourself with says something about your choices and impacts your happiness. *Surround yourself with the good!*

#5: Your limitations are set by you! If I asked you what your ultimate dream is, what would you say? Is it a big dream? Would others get excited about it? Does it energize you every day? Now if I asked you that same question, but this time I told you you're guaranteed to reach that dream, would your dream be the same dream or a more ambitious one? Of course, it would be more ambitious, because you were sure you couldn't fail. Right?

The truth is that too often, when you try to think big, you allow your inner bully to hold you back. It plants thoughts in your mind. "That could never happen," or, "Be realistic!" or, "You'll never be able to do that!" The question I ask you is: *Why do you allow your inner bully to limit your dreams?* Don't let it! Don't limit yourself! The best way to break through limitations is to remain determined, continue actions that move you closer to your goals and stop listening to your inner bully. Instead of thinking, "I don't think I can do that," you must think, "I can totally do that!" Instead of thinking, "That's impossible," say, "That has so many possibilities!" You become limitless when you allow your dreams to be big, followed by a positive, optimistic attitude, and action. *Dream big!*

#6: Your family is very important even if they drive you nuts! Yes, that's what I said! Even though your sister or brother, or your parents seem intolerable at times, they are a part of you and have had a large part in molding the person you are, whether you want to admit it or not. The father who is always there and the father that missed everything; *yup!* Both are equally significant in influencing your life today. The mom that loved every inch of you and the mother that critiqued every last bit of you are equally important. The siblings that you never had and the siblings that nagged at, laughed with, picked on, and played with you, all play a huge part in your present life.

There is a lesson learned from each family member you have had or never met. Be thankful for the wisdom they afforded you. *Look for the lessons!*

#7: Sleep is extremely important to your overall health and success, and it can never be "made up!" You need your sleep on a regular basis. The worst thing you can do is to skimp where sleep is concerned. Lack of sleep affects your days in ways far beyond what you would guess!

Your lack of energy at the office after a poor night's sleep or the impatience with your kids after a night of restlessness is only the tip of the iceberg. The careless mistake you make on a memo, the yawns in front of your coworkers or your boss, not to mention the biological increase of your stress hormone, cortisol, are all symptomatic of sleep deprivation. Lack of sleep will kick your butt and sabotage your success. A good night's sleep beneficially impacts your bottom line as well as your waistline. I say that you can't "make up" a sleep deficit because you can never make up the hours and incidents of poor performance caused by the lack of proper, rejuvenating, restful sleep. *Make your sleep environment a sanctuary!*

#8: Eat healthfully to restore your body's energy and minimize illness! How you treat your body says a lot about how you treat other aspects of your life. It's amazing how quickly we run to the doctor to be given a pill for a headache, for acne, to rid ourselves of some unwanted weight, or feelings of sadness. We assume we're ill because of stress caused by deadlines, our age, a stressful ex, or the neighbor's barking dog. Yet we forget to ask ourselves, *what did I put in my body today?* The human body has an amazing ability to heal itself if you just get out of the way and let it.

Give every cell the opportunity to restore and rejuvenate by ingesting proper nutritional whole foods and lots of water. Your happiness and success will only be as optimal as your physical health. Don't be lazy with your health unless you want a lazy life. *Eat to nourish your body!*

#9: Live your life *wholistically*! The key to successful *wholism* is to address all the aspects of your life every single day. All too often, you approach only one aspect of your life to improve upon. Some of you approach losing weight, or a new relationship, or the need to make more money as your only focus. You cannot turn your back on any one area of your life to work on another single area. You must be ready to juggle it all and you will learn how in the pages ahead. *Everything is connected!*

#10: Stop your inner bully! Perhaps the most insidious thing you do that keeps you from reaching your full potential is letting the bully within you run wild. You allow the negative thoughts your inner bully feeds you to control every aspect of your life. I will teach you how to reprogram your brain to save you from thoughts and actions dictated by your inner bully. Most importantly, once you identify your personal inner bully and knock it down, you'll thrive. *You will control your inner bully!*

Get ready to learn more from my life rules in the pages ahead. Are you ready? We have a lot of work to do!

> *"Every moment I shape my destiny with a chisel.*
> *I am a carpenter of my own soul."*
> −RUMI

Your Song, Your Dance

Before we dive further in, I need you to do something for yourself. Think of your life as it is right now and ask yourself, "If my life were a song that played along with my present life-dance, how would that song sound? What would that song say? What would my dance and song be like joined together?"

Write this out:

Title of your song:

_____

Rhythm/Tempo: (Fast, Slow, Choppy)

_____

Genre of your song: (Jazz, Blues, Country, Pop, etc.)

_____

What would your chorus/hook line in your song say?

_____

What type of movie would your song be played in?

_____

You will come back to this at the end of the book!

"There is a need to find and sing our own song, to stretch our limbs and shake them in a dance so wild that nothing can roost there, that stirs the yearning for solitary voyage."
–BARBARA LAZEAR ASCHER

Connect & Be Aware

Be Whole, Be Wholistic

You know some new rules to live by and you have thrown out some of the negative trash in your life, now ultimately, to truly be successful in defeating your internal bully you need to strive towards what I call *"wholism,"* because you need to be a *whole* person. And the word *"wholistic"* marries the words whole and holistic. It is the practice of holistic medicine that treats the *whole* person. You need to treat your *whole* self in order to live a healthy, happy life, free of self-destructive thoughts and negativity. The inner bully cannot survive the *wholistic* environment. At the end of the day, you need to be emotionally healthy, physically healthy, spiritually healthy, financially healthy, and healthy in your relationships with everyone, including the paramount relationship with yourself.

Does this sound like a lot? If your answer is, "No, I can do this," you're on the right track. *Start everything with a positive attitude.* If, on the other hand, your answer is, "How can I possibly work on all of this?" I will show you how to give your life the *whole* approach. Remember, everything is connected (Life Rule #9 above). You must be ready to juggle it all!

"Change will not come if we wait for some other person or some other time. We are the ones we've been waiting for. We are the change we seek!"
–AUTHOR UNKNOWN

When I was fifteen pounds heavier, my stress level was high. My personal relationships were a disaster. My financial situation was the only area of my life that was not in total chaos; however, because I viewed everything negatively, I also viewed my finances as being in disarray. Why? Because I was not taking care of my *whole* self and the only thing I focused on was my desire to lose weight, believing that alone would make me happy. Yup! I was being a *reductionist* (more on this later). I thought that if I worked on my weight loss alone, all of the other areas in my life would just get better. *That was wishful thinking and it didn't work!*

Instead of letting the idea of losing weight saturate my mind, I decided I needed to take the *wholistic* approach and work on all aspects of my life. I needed to focus on all the positive things around me. I needed to pick up the phone and connect with people to build up my relationships. I needed to take time to breathe and say nice things to myself every day. I needed to smile more at work, even when I didn't particularly feel like it. I needed to prepare healthy meals and take control of what I was putting in my mouth rather than eating at a drive-through. And I definitely needed to take control of the dysfunctional messages that were going through my mind and coming out of my mouth. I was being negative and therefore attracting negative people. My relationships were not healthy because I was not healthy. I was not treating myself with respect, so I was attracting disrespectful people. I was not nurturing my *whole* life. I was not trying to juggle it *all*; therefore satisfying weight loss was not possible.

"To enjoy life, we must touch much of it lightly."
–VOLTAIRE

End the Reductionist Approach

Our society is big on *reductionism,* tending to deal with things in their simplest form in all aspects of life. As a result of this reductionist approach, your view of things in general tends to be compartmentalized. This may at times be more efficient, but it is not always in your best interests. We are complex beings and we need to work on the complexity of our *whole* lives.

As an example of this reductionist approach, a reductionist doctor will tell his cancer patient, "We'll cut out the tumor, give you radiation and/or chemotherapy treatments and then check your blood count every few months to keep an eye on things." Does that seem to be a complete enough treatment? What about the nutritional needs of a cancer patient? Should the level of physical activity remain the same? Should the stress levels in the patient's daily life be examined? What about their need for positive relationships? What about the patient's mindset in general, his or her attitude towards the disease? What about living and care arrangements? Will the patient have any spiritual connection through this process? As you can see, reductionism treats only the cancerous tumor and not the *whole* patient.

Minimizing everything and giving everything and everyone a limiting function is all around us. Reductionism is in the workplace. We classify individuals and ensure they adhere to their job descriptions: custodians, secretaries, middle management, upper management, executives, and the CEO. Reducing people down to their job title in this reductionist society tends to distance individual employees from the entirety of the company. When a company I worked for was under attack, many employees reacted as if the attack had nothing to do with them. At a certain point, people whom we've reduced down experience a disconnect to the whole enchilada! Rather than reducing aspects of life, you should be enhancing your life with the all-inclusive approach I call, *wholism,* where everything is connected. Focusing on only one aspect of your life can be very misleading.

A scientist I follow, T. Colin Campbell, PhD, once gave an example of reductionism in terms of an apple. He talked about how the apple, as a whole, is truly more beneficial for us than just the individual nutrients that make up the apple. Take the valuable vitamin C in the whole apple; scientists put the vitamin C, in a capsule and say, "Here you are. You can have your vitamin C without eating the apple." *Reductionist!* Dr. Campbell has found that the vitamin C in the capsule, although it may be a thousand milligrams more vitamin C than what is available in the apple, doesn't act the same in your body as the vitamin C within the apple. You see your body needs the whole apple. The whole apple has the zinc, copper, fiber, magnesium, potassium, enzymes, electrolytes, and much more, as well as the vitamin C. All the properties of the apple work in harmony for your body to utilize the vitamin C most efficiently, along with all the other healthy properties in the whole apple. Likewise, a company cannot flourish if one classification of people feels encapsulated and disconnected from the others. Everyone matters. The whole organization is needed if it is to succeed just as the whole apple is needed for your body to properly utilize the disease fighting properties of the vitamin C. The same goes for every aspect of your life, everything matters, and you need it all.

Are you a reductionist? If you are, you will blame your unraveling life on one thing, perhaps your finances. Substitute, "I need to make more money," with, "I need to be more responsible with the money that I have." If you truly want to make more money you need to put action behind that thought and look at how you are leaking money in **all** aspects of your life. Your money issues are not just impacted by the amount of money on the check that your boss signs, they're impacted by every aspect of your *whole* life.

You see it is never just one thing. You must look at how your money is utilized in all aspects of your life. You have greater control over how you spend then on how much money you make.

If your approach to your life is to always work on one thing independently of all else, you are going to cause stress in your life. You need to have a healthy influence in your personal life, in your financial life, in your physical life, and in your professional life (worksheets to use in charting your progress follow the text) for satisfying change to occur. If you do not approach weight loss in a *whole* way you may be left wondering why you are still not satisfied even if you do lose weight. You need to approach every category in your life with a little effort every day for satisfying weight loss to occur or whatever your goals may be. When you approach each category in your life with mindfulness and purposeful action every day, you start moving towards a more *happy-whole-you!*

My journey to a healthy, *wholistic* life began when I stopped focusing solely on weight loss to create happiness and began working on my own personal development and growth. You see I was unhappy, but I tied my happiness to my weight (reductionist approach). Consequently, "If I lost the weight, I would be happy." This was so not true. Therefore, I started replacing poor habits with helpful habits in every area of my life. I called this the add-in method (more on this later).

Instead of listening to music in my car, I replaced that habit with listening to personal development CDs. Instead of staying at my desk on my breaks, I started taking walks every day and started breathing deeper to clear my mind to reduce stress. I started building my relationships. I started to pray, listen to the positive music, and acknowledge a higher Being, which nurtured my spiritual side. I chose to give myself positive daily affirmations and think about all the things I was thankful for before turning in for the night. I resolved to buy healthier food and save money by not eating out. I began to get massages and take time for me. I stopped paying attention to the scale. I stopped comparing myself to others. I did a little of all of this every day. By changing my reductionist focus of weight loss, *"Exercise a ton and eat very little,"* I changed it to a more *wholistic* approach with an, *"Everything matters and can improve my overall desires,"* attitude, my whole life improved. Every aspect of my life became more satisfying and I became happier. My bank account grew; my relationships grew deeper; my stress level was lowered; I enjoyed my job more; and I even lost the fifteen pounds. I was becoming *whole* by practicing *wholism*. I created a new reality for myself by working on all aspects of my life simultaneously. A little bit all the time, it is never just one thing!

You need to stop trying to find the magic bullet, the miracle in a pill, the one investment that will make you millions, the one person that will make you truly happy or the one workout machine that will lose the weight for you. It is not just choosing to buy that new exercise machine that will improve your health; you must also use it, you must also eat healthfully, you must have positive thoughts, you must get your rest, manage your time better— and you must work on all of these things. It is when you act on all aspects of your life; physical health, nutritional health, mental health, spiritual health, your relationships, and your occupational health that you will start getting compound results that will improve your overall well-being. You must work on it all. *Eat the whole apple. It all matters!*

> *"Every time you are tempted to react in the same old way,*
> *ask yourself if you want to be a prisoner of the past or a*
> *pioneer of the future."*
> –DEEPAK CHOPRA

You need to make decisions based on your *whole* self, and on your *whole* environment. The possibility of approaching your life from this *wholistic* standpoint may perhaps feel unattainable, but it is anything but! You may be thinking that you can't focus on your physical, nutritional, mental, financial health, and relationships all at once. But it will only *feel* like it is too much to focus on all at once, if you approach each area with the idea that you have to perfect them all equally, but you don't. You can work on losing weight, while spending less money, work on improving your mindset and eliminating any negative outer sources all at once. This creates a movement towards a better *whole* life, which I call… you guessed it… *wholism.*

It is the compilation of all the good and bad choices you make in every area of your life that will make you feel as if your life is either successful or crumbling apart. I believe a healthy mind is a healthy heart. A healthy heart is a healthy soul. A healthy soul is a healthy life. A healthy life is a happy life. A happy life is a successful life.

Remember, you don't have to find a "perfect" balance. *Wholism* is not about perfection; it's about participation in every aspect of your life. You are juggling each aspect every day, dancing to connect every aspect of your life with another aspect. The important thing is to activate all areas of your life without abandoning any area. Some areas may need more work; other areas may have more ups and downs. But the goal is to be mindful of each area in your life and put effort into them all. You may be sprinting forward with your weight loss, skipping along improving your diet, dancing with improving your pessimistic mindset, and crawling forward with your finances. That's good! The most important thing here is you are improving and moving in every area. The Happy-Whole-You Daily graphics following this text (worksheet #2) will assist you in keeping track of your progress in these areas. As you move forward towards your goals, at whatever pace, set your goals high and refer back to all aspects of the Happy-Whole-You Matrix (worksheet #3). Let the matrixes throughout this book be a reminder of what you need to juggle and connect (look for worksheet #3 in the pages ahead).

You are programmed to be a reductionist. Do you accept others giving you a reductionist approach in life? Do you approach your life focusing on only one thing at a time? Are you a reductionist? You must look at the whole picture and fight having that reductionist mentality. Just imagine if a math class was being taught as a cooking class, a shopping class, a physical fitness class, and a reading class all in one. Wouldn't that be great? Do you use math in any of these areas? Absolutely! Yet we teach math as if it were just numbers and signs on a piece of paper separated from real life. Think of areas in your life that you address with a "reductionist" approach. What are they? It might be your work life, your poor spending habits, or a toxic relationship you're in. How can those areas in your life be improved by connecting them to other areas of your life? Write your answers below.

Reductionist area:

How can I recruit other areas of my life to help me in this area?

If you truly want to end the reductionist approach and need support with this, look into the Happy-Whole-You coaching programs or other coaching programs. Having a certified coach can help you discover your best-self and create the life you have always wanted. I coach individuals with my *wholistic* approach, an everything matters and is interconnected approach.

> *"The whole is greater than the sum of its parts."*
> −ARISTOTLE

Worksheet #2—The Daily Activity Matrix

This second worksheet is your Happy-Whole-You Daily sheet, which provides you with a visual window into every aspect of your life. You'll be nurturing them daily and end the reductionist approach. To use this worksheet, place a dot on every sector of the YOU circle and think about how often you nurture this Happy-Whole-You Daily activity. Place a dot on the *outermost* piece of any section you attend to daily (such as a fitness routine). If you're not consistent with any one activity (such as reciting your daily affirmations), put your dot in the *middle* of that piece. If you haven't yet put energy into an activity (such as paying it forward) put your dot closest to the center of the pie. Once you're done with each sector of the pie, connect your dots. You will probably not make a perfect circle at first; however, over time you want the connected dots on your Daily Matrix to look more and more like a circle. You can use the same worksheet daily, using different color ink monthly to mark your dots, and compare your circles over time. Be sure to make a key with the color and date, for proper tracking of your progress.

www.HappyWholeYou.com

Avoid Autopilot

Now you know that everything matters and moving forward I must warn you about being on autopilot. During your life, you may sometimes go on autopilot. It happens to the best of us. To explain what I mean by "going on autopilot," I am going to again analogize your life as a dance. You start living on autopilot when your dance steps become easy and comfortable and you find yourself dancing, but you've forgotten how you got to that point. Your feet are moving, life is passing you by, and you may be feeling mediocre—maybe even happy—but then all of a sudden, BAM! You trip, look around and wonder how you got here? You forget your next step; you forget where you were. You were bored and not really paying full attention to what you're doing. You begin to feel confused, and you have slowed down. You feel weighed down, like you're burdened with hundreds of pounds on your back. What happened? You were moving along just fine. Now, you can barely put one foot in front of the other and your dance comes to a stop; your life seems to be at a standstill and you have no idea how you have gotten to where you are. You are not happy!

When you're experiencing positive events in your life, it is as if you're learning new dance steps. Your attention is on new strategies, your attention is enhanced as you're working on your new masterpiece performance and you are excited. You're growing and feeling strong. But after a while when the newness wears off, you ease up and stop making progress. That's when you stop learning. After all, you have perfected your new masterpiece! When it becomes easy for you and you start coasting endlessly and almost mindlessly performing the same steps without having to think about them, you've stopped growing. You are no longer energizing yourself by learning new steps. You've stopped challenging yourself. You're back on autopilot. This can happen at your job, in your home life, in your spiritual life, with your health, in your relationships, in any aspect you find yourself just going through the motions after the newness wears off.

I call the time between our highs and lows the meantime. This is when you are coasting along with a sense of calmness and have stopped growing. This meantime space is a great place to get to because it affords you a pleasing sense of comfort. The problem arises when you stay in this meantime space too long. Have you ever noticed that someone will work very hard to get a new job, learn all their new duties, and then, when they've become comfortable in it, they simply go through the motions? They stop learning new things. They're on autopilot and the, "in the meantime," has taken over their lifetime.

You usually go on autopilot when you've experienced a substantial amount of space between the attention-grabbing negative events in your life (needing a job) and the captivating, positive events in your life (finding a job and learning to do it so well it becomes second nature). The space of time between the negative and the positive events can be comforting but it causes us to fall asleep at the wheel. Our attention span goes dormant. The inner bully is ready to surprise you when this happens. This is the phenomenon that sometimes happens in a relationship and results in taking someone's presence and even their love, for granted.

You must keep learning new dance steps and challenging yourself. Keep things fresh and new! You are welcoming the inner bully with open arms when you stop pushing yourself to new levels. You become bored and bitter. You become negative and complacent. You become the unmotivated person who starts to complain a lot, gain weight, and has no energy. Don't allow this to happen!

> *"Success is a journey, not a destination. It requires constant effort, vigilance, and reevaluation."*
> –MARK TWAIN

The tricky thing about finding yourself on autopilot is you start to feel weighed down when this happens and it happens very fast. You were living life; dancing with a smile for days, weeks, and even months, then boom! Your serenity turned to restlessness. Your sense of comfort morphed into distress. Your dance tripped into a slow, boring walk. What happened? When you got into your comfort zone, the "meantime" space you started to coast along, the inner bully got the message that you had taken your eye off of growth. The inner bully wanted to come out and play and saw the chance to do exactly that. So, without much mindfulness during this time of supposed serenity and ease, your inner bully started influencing you, first in teeny-tiny ways. You abandoned your inner motivation to learn new dance steps, new skills. You stopped pushing forward with hard work and you became complacent, comfortable, and stagnant. This scenario happens more often than you think.

We are all creatures of habit and we therefore love our repetitive daily patterns and comfort.

You interrupt these daily patterns in a positive way when you begin to build something new in your life: a new home, a family, a new job or career. You grow substantially during these times. However, when you do nothing more, you take your eye off of growing and building your masterpiece and you simply go through the motions and get comfortable. Then one day you look in the mirror and ask yourself, "How did I get here? How did things get so off track?" You've caught yourself on autopilot. You stopped making the little adjustments and setting new goals. You got comfortable coasting along, and that led to finding yourself confused and out of alignment. You started off so strong! But then, you stopped improving yourself and you stopped doing the things that kept you moving toward your goals. The inner bully was right by your side when you first hit autopilot and entered the "meantime" zone. The inner bully comforted you during that time, lulling you with songs telling you that everything was okay; after all, you'd done so much! You had a job, a house, and a car, no need to work on yourself anymore. You did it! Did what? Are you truly successful and happy? Is there ever an end point for happiness and success? Happiness and success only evolve when you evolve. There is no ceiling. There is so much more to life when you continue to push and challenge yourselves.

> *"If everything seems under control, you're not going fast enough."*
> –MARIO ANDRETTI

Unfortunately, in this autopilot "meantime" zone you move backward. The negative voice of your inner bully gets stronger as you start to realize you don't really want to be on autopilot anymore. You start questioning your state of calm because you realize you're not moving forward and meanwhile, the inner bully is growing inwardly and starts to influence you. So, you begin having feelings of boredom and guilt. You start feeling weighed down and depressed because you're not improving your current state. You then indulge the inner bully by making some relatively small but poor decisions. At the time these bad decisions don't seem like much to you but they quickly weigh you down and empower your inner bully. As more bully moments accrue, the weight on you accumulates, dragging you down further.

When this starts to happen, you find yourself saying self-destructive things like, "My life sucks," or, "I look tired and fat," or, "My job is so boring," or, "I'm just sick and tired of everything," or, "Why is everything wrong?" or, "What did I do to deserve this?" Every time you say or do a negative bully thing at this juncture, picture yourself throwing a ten-pound weight on your back. You have to carry this weight around with you everywhere you go, at home, at work, at church and anywhere else you venture. Get ready to start adding up the pounds or you can simply get rid of the bully inside you!

At work, you might tell yourself that a co-worker or a client doesn't like you; or perhaps you think your boss prefers someone else to you. This thought adds another ten pounds onto your back. Then you scold yourself because you're sure you'll never make that work deadline. Follow this with picking a fight with your spouse or a friend, because you are feeling so stressed; add another ten pounds and another ten pounds. Before bed, you drink two or three glasses of wine instead of the usual one glass. Add ten more pounds to that. You start surfing the web more and comparing how happy people's Facebook pages look compared to your life. Add ten more pounds! You let your diet revert back to junk food instead of making healthy food choices. Add another ten pounds. You are too busy and too stressed to connect with your friends so you stop all contact with them. Add ten more pounds. Then you start comparing the house you have, the car you drive, and the clothes you wear to everyone else. You start to think things are not fair, ten more pounds please, and the stress continues. You only exercise two days a week, if at all, in place of the four days a week you were committed to because "it's hopeless," or, "you'll get back on track tomorrow," or, "you don't want to be seen at the gym until you lose the extra weight." Add ten pounds. You start staying up late watching TV to "clear your mind" which cuts your sleep short, another ten pounds. And so, the pounds keep adding up over time. This all began with being complacent, being on autopilot. The snowball effect is in full force!

"Even if you're on the right track, you'll get run over
if you just sit there."
–WILL ROGERS

As you can see, it is never just one big thing that weighs you down. It's all the little choices you make while on autopilot, over an extended period of time that make you carry an ever-heavier load, leaving you emotionally drained. The added problem is that as you become weaker and more fatigued from all this additional weight you're carrying, you become far more vulnerable to your inner bully. Your emotional state becomes as fragile as a cracked egg. You're not broken yet, but as soon as you get jostled by the next life event, you'll crack more and ooze everywhere. You are a mess! You can't take one more bump in the road. When you're fragile, any change that comes your way will break you easily like the egg that is already cracked. When you are, weak and weighed down, all it takes is something like a car accident, a job loss, a divorce, or even a positive event, like a pregnancy, promotion, engagement, or wedding to put you flat on your face, oozing tears. All the weight you were already carrying just doubled and you feel like you cannot move forward another step. This new weight hits you like a ton of bricks. You cannot handle it. You stop dancing.

The lesson here is two-fold. First, you cannot stop improving yourself and working hard or your inner bully will come out. The second lesson is that it is not the "big" event like the wedding or the job loss alone that will flatten you. It is all the little stuff along the way that adds up and pushes you down as a result of your choices.

Here are a few things you can add to your day for continued personal growth:

1. Take 10 minutes every morning to read something positive or watch something positive;

2. Add a positive app on your phone that sends you positive daily messages;

3. Add a notification on your computer to go off every hour to get you moving. Every time you hear it stand up stretch, go for a brisk walk or do some squats. Just move!

4. Before you go to bed, write down three things you want to work on the next day;

5. Right now, write down everything you want to accomplish in your lifetime and post it somewhere close by;

6. Have someone who can support and motivate you to contact you daily or weekly.

7. Get a coach. Someone to hold you accountable and push you to be your best-self.

8. Join the Happy-Whole-You community to connect and be inspired.

> *"Make sure you are only carrying today's burdens.*
> *Too often we carry far more than necessary.*
> *Reduce your load by dropping tomorrow's worries,*
> *and yesterday's baggage.*
> *Present pressures and problems are usually enough.*
> *Leave tomorrow's until later."*
> –PATRICK LINDSAY

Everything is Connected

You have to act *wholistically,* continuously working on all aspects of your life for things to work out and get better, as we have discussed. Whether you are aware of it or not, there exists a continuous inner connection between every aspect of your life. You can't have a bad work life and think that your bad work life will not weigh you down in your personal life. You can't exercise regularly but eat a bad diet and wonder why you aren't losing weight or why you're tired all the time. You can't gossip and speak poorly about other people and expect others to speak in high regard about you. You can't neglect your spouse and relationships and expect your marriage and social life to be vibrant. You can't hold on to past mistakes or grudges and expect to be worry-free. You must let go of the negative. Every piece of your life is valuable. Every relationship, every thought you have, every bad habit and every good habit matters. How you choose to respond, how you choose to think, how you choose to love, all matter. *Everything is connected!* If you are neglecting one area of life, like your relationships or physical health or your spiritual well-being or your work life—whatever it may be—you are "adding weight" in *all* aspects of your life.

Here's an example of how I allowed things to snowball in my life and allowed my inner bully to dominate me. I let the stresses from a problematic relationship keep me up at night, which caused me to sleep-in the next morning and skip my morning workout. Because I skipped my morning workout, I lacked energy all day and stressed the entire day because I keep thinking that I needed to fit in time for a workout before the day's end. But by 5:00 p.m., I was too tired and too hungry to workout, so I decided to skip my daily workout (for the second time) and I told myself I would start my workout routine the next day. So, I went home, grabbed a quick unhealthy bite to eat, lay down on the couch, put my feet up, and turned on the TV. I felt guilty about my lack of exercise, my poor dinner choices, and my messy house. I tried to decompress by watching television. A few times, I thought of getting up to clean the house a bit, but before I knew it, the clock read 10:30 p.m. and I was exhausted. I stayed on the couch mindlessly watching TV for another hour or so, knowing I needed to be up at 4:30 a.m. the next morning in order to get my morning workout in and get my kids ready for school with a healthy breakfast in their bellies, or else have another day like the one I'd just had. And then I thought, *hmm… maybe I should take the day off from work tomorrow to catch up on my sleep, clean the house, do the laundry and get some personal things done.* Does this sound like you? Have you ever had to miss life, take a day off of work or miss a fun event because you were just too tired and stressed out due to something that kept you up one night and started your snowball effect?

Substitute whatever keeps you up at night or throws you off track, for my problematic relationship and the cycle I described may look similar. All aspects of your life matter and each aspect impacts the other aspects. Be mindful of the extra weight you may be carrying around from your decisions.

Another example of this snowball effect occurs when you lose your job. It may feel like a ton of bricks hit you and flattened you out. You feel like you are road kill, as you're lying flat on the ground feeling defeated. But while you're on the ground cursing your boss (as if they were the one that caused this) you must realize that the bottom line is that you are the reason you're lying on the ground. Anytime the snowball effect is in play it is because of your choices. All the little decisions and choices you made up until that very moment were already weighing you down, making you fragile, but you let it happen. You were already cracking. If you hadn't already been making small, poor choices that added pounds of stress to you, most likely you'd still be able to stand up tall despite the impact of a job loss. Or perhaps, you wouldn't have even lost your job if you had been mindful and continually been involved with improving yourself and moving forward in life.

It is our nature to blame the last thing that came along for having flattened us out, but in reality, it was all the small choices you made day-in and day-out that you must recognize and take ownership of that kicked your butt.

Let's go back to the job loss, which left you lying flat on the ground cursing your boss. What if you had been more positive at work? What if you had done a little extra and never complained? What if you were always on time, showed up with a smile on your face and an open ear to listen? What if you chose not to gossip and when you heard others gossiping you kindly changed the subject? You could have even eliminated yourself from associating with gossipers. Maybe your job loss was completely out of your control. Maybe your company shut down. Maybe your company moved to another area. If you have been in a situation where there were layoffs and your company was not doing well, what could you have done during the anticipation of the layoff? Could you have been looking for another job? Could you have spoken to your boss to see what more you could do? Could you have asked your boss for a referral to another company? Were you saving your money to ensure you have six to twelve months of savings in case the job loss happened? You had a lot of choices! You always have a choice.

We could ponder a lot of "what-ifs" that may or may not have led to the job loss. Maybe the job loss wouldn't have been as devastating "if." But it holds true that you will always be able to handle unexpected life events with more grace, if you haven't been beating yourself up and weighing yourself down along the way.

As we discussed earlier, you can find yourself feeling happy and dancing along like everything is great, for a moment, a day, or a few months, and then all of a sudden (or at least it may seem like it's sudden) you find yourself running on autopilot. You stop making all the small positive choices. You start slowing down and begin feeling heavy. Feelings of sadness, feelings of less-than, and feelings of being unsuccessful and feelings of frustration start to creep in until you find yourself off track, wondering how you got there. If you have ever experienced these emotions and found yourself weakened, broken and flattened, you must remember that this started when your internal bully quietly and slowly began taking over and influencing you to make tiny poor choices. You became complacent and stopped paying attention and your gloating inner bully smiled and took your hand. Don't allow this to happen!

List three very detailed negative events in which you felt like a ton of bricks got thrown on your back, flattened you, and you felt you were road kill. What had you been doing until the point that the "something big" hit? In other words, what were the little ten-pound weights in your life that kept adding up?

Big negative events:

1.

2.

3.

All the little ten-pound weights:

Event 1	Event 2	Event 3
1.	1.	1.
2.	2.	2.
3.	3.	3.
4.	4.	4.
5…	5…	5…

Do you notice any patterns within your little ten-pound weights that kept adding up? How does this make you feel?

Describe below:

As you think back through these events and times, at what moment or at what single action did you begin to sabotage yourself? Where did the first of the many ten-pound weights you carried start? You need to realize that every outcome in your life begins with a thought followed by an action. What was the thought that caused you to get that first ten-pound weight? You need to be able to go back and identify this moment, and work through it so that you can make sense of where you are now. If you could go back in time to that moment, what would you do differently? What would you say differently?

You must learn from your past and keep moving forward towards your future. The lesson you learn is a silver lining that lies behind every event you experience, both the good and the bad. When you find the silver lining behind a given event, you can begin to move forward towards growth as a more, well-rounded *whole* person. Let's be honest. If we can't see the good and grow from all the foolish things we put ourselves through, aren't we back to where we started? Aren't we still bullying ourselves? Good comes from growth. It's easy to fall back into that autopilot, ugly state, and think toward the negative, but there is positive in all events, even those you perceive as being negative. If you allow yourself to find the positive and learn from it, you'll excel towards a better future. You must stop reacting to life and allow yourself to respond properly.

"The soul should always stand ajar, ready to welcome the ecstatic experience."

–EMILY DICKINSON

Reflect

Learn from Your Past, Own Your Future

All of us have an incredible past, and sometimes, to move forward, we must reflect back. The differences in our past experiences give each of us a unique approach in our lives and our past experiences house valuable lesson for our future growth. I want to share a little about my own past dance with you. I struggled with self-acceptance from a very young age. I've always been hard on myself and because of this, many exciting accomplishments I had were quickly overshadowed by thoughts that what I'd done was not good enough and that I should have done better. I was depressed. I lacked true happiness and the inner bully loves to lead a dance with someone who is unhappy.

These negative feelings began between the ages of eight and ten. How many kids label themselves as depressed at that age? Not a lot. If you'd asked me, I wouldn't have said that I was depressed; I would have said I felt I was "different from other kids." I remember feeling that I wasn't good enough. This feeling of inadequacy continued into my adulthood, despite all the objectively wonderful things I did and all that I had in my life. Let me share a bit about my childhood with you so you'll understand.

I grew up in an old farmhouse with a giant backyard in Charlotte (shar-LOT), a very nice, small community of about 9,000 people outside of Lansing, Michigan. My parents had five children. I have three older siblings and a younger sibling.

My oldest brother was a night owl who had turned a large closet in our farmhouse into his DJ room where he would spin records wearing his big headphones late into the night and whenever I had a nightmare—which was often—I would crawl into his "studio," curl up on the floor, and just watch him until I fell back asleep. (He actually started a DJ business in junior high.)

One year, my dad had a small garage on our property demolished and, as a family we built a big pole barn, the size of a three-car garage. My DJ brother—with help from Dad—built a DJ booth overlooking that large garage where he'd have dances. He would stream the rafters with lights and it seemed like every teenaged kid in town would be there. I loved it so much; I'd sneak into the barn to dance with the big kids every chance I got.

My sister, five years older than me, had always been my role model, though I'd never tell her. Ironically, she was my complete opposite. She was blond, whereas I'm a brunette. She was a cheerleader in high school and full of self-confidence. Attempting to follow in her footsteps, I was a cheerleader for a few years, but then realized I'd rather be on the football team, playing tackle football with the boys. For an entire year, I begged my mom to let me join the football team and she finally caved in and allowed it! To everyone's surprise, I was good! After every game, I'd take my helmet off, shake out my long brown hair, and, with a big smile on my face, shake hands with the boys on the opposing team. I remember the look on their faces when they realized I was a girl. How could I ever forget their astonishment? Doubtless, it was a very cool experience, but it left me feeling tomboyish. I liked boys and I knew boys wouldn't want to take a girl who could knock them over on the football field on a date. My sister came to my rescue. She taught me how to do my hair. I'm talking 80s and early 90s, big Aqua Net hairspray hair. If I went outside in a typhoon, not a single hair on my head would move. My sister also taught me how to shave my legs and how to match clothes. She even made me a *New Kids on the Block* shirt when I couldn't afford to buy one. My campfire group was going to a New Kids concert and all the other kids were wearing one. My sister took a white T-shirt and with bright, puffy paint had written, Donnie, Jordan, Joey, Jonathan, and Danny on the shirt. I was so excited to feel like I fit in with the other girls! She was really good to me even though, as her younger sister, I know I was often an annoyance to her.

One of my brothers, two years older than me, was fun to play with because he was always up to something. We liked to play board games, especially, Monopoly. He always beat my younger brother and me. He was a natural and I think this game helped him develop his excellent entrepreneurial skills from a young age. He was always looking for ways to earn money. He would dig up worms and sell them. He collected coins and would make deals and trade them. He would mow lawns for cash and help my parents sell picnic tables for a commission (for extra money my mom and dad would sell redwood picnic tables in our front yard. We could earn $100 for every table we sold). He was a born businessman. He even got my younger brother and me to help him with almost anything he wanted—without pay. But I had fun being part of his ventures. To me, they were adventures.

My youngest brother and I were the babies. We were always poking our noses in everyone else's business. We would ride our bikes three to four miles to elementary school and back together. We had to ride our bikes because I'd been kicked off the bus numerous times for disorderly conduct. Yup, I was a handful! I was thankful for my little brother's company on our bike commutes. We played well together and my other brother, who was two years older, often played with us. We were a threesome. The problem with a group of three kids is that inevitably, one is always left out. That someone was always my younger brother or me. Our older brother and I would lock our baby brother out of the house for hours. He'd be so upset; he'd go banging on every door. We thought it was hysterical! They did the same thing to me. Our parents left us home alone often and we were constantly fighting, playing, fighting and playing. But as much as we would fight at home, I always had my little brother's back in school and was always so proud of him. Having a younger brother allowed me to feel like I had someone to look after and play with.

We were not a wealthy family, but there was always love in our home and a sibling there to pick your spirits up or trip you up. Our old house provided an awesome platform for adventures. We had railroad tracks along the back of our property and we'd set pennies on the tracks when we heard a train coming. Those pennies would flatten like pancakes. On the other side of the tracks, was a public golf course. My siblings and I would jump the tracks and sneak onto the course to find golf balls. A small creek flowed alongside the course, so finding golf balls in the mucky creek was a sure thing. We'd slide down the slopes to the water and our shoes and socks would always get soaking wet, but it was worth it to score a ball. I loved finding the pink ones. When we'd secured enough balls, we'd run and hide next to a ball-cleaning station until the coast was clear. Then we'd wash as many of the balls as we could and run back under the bridge, hoping not to get caught. We would repeat this until we had cleaned every spot off the golf balls. Returning home, we were excited to show Mom our stash. She'd give us egg cartons and my older brother—the entrepreneur—would put the balls in egg cartons and sell a dozen of them for $5.00 alongside with his worms.

Another fun thing I did in my childhood was to ride my bike down the path that ran parallel to the railroad tracks. The three-mile path was overgrown with trees and shrubs. It felt like I was riding through a forest. Bugs would hit my face with such force! The worst was when I would get a bug in my eye! But the path led to town and I'd ride my bike as fast as I could down that path. The freedom to travel to town and back on my "secret" path, as a kid was so cool! It gave me a real sense of independence.

Then there was our neighbor's pool where we could swim anytime. But with this freedom came responsibilities. To earn our stay, we had to help vacuum the pool and skim the bugs out. I remember there were some summer days when I would swim for so long that when I finally got out of the pool I was starving and my stomach was aching. My fingers and toes were shriveled up like raisins. I would sprint home and beg my mom for something to eat. The best was when she had slices of watermelon and tiny peanut butter and jelly sandwiches cut in fourths ready and waiting for me. I would slow down just enough to devour as many as I could.

Our big circular driveway afforded us an opportunity to have a little competition. It was large enough to serve as an awesome spot to have bike races and play basketball. Not so enjoyable, was waking up during the winter months to see that driveway covered with snow we had to shovel away. It was so early and always so dark and cold. I hated that chore, but we had to do it because my mom ran a daycare center, so every morning at 6:30 a.m. kids would start showing up at my house. When I got home from school, the kids were still there.

As you can see, our home was always full of exciting activities and I had a great childhood filled with adventure. I always had something to do and there were always kids around. My parents were very loving and always there for us. So how is it that I still had this yucky feeling inside me, a sort of sadness that wouldn't go away?

"If you have a family that loves you, food on the table, clothes on
your back, and a roof over your head, you are richer than many!"
–UNKNOWN

My Inner Bully is Born

All of you have had a moment in your past when the inner bully grabbed your happiness-meter and took control of how you felt about yourself and the world around you. This moment changed the set of your sail in life. You were, no doubt, not aware of what it was, when it was happening, and how it has changed you. Could this have happened when your parents went through a divorce? When you lost a loved one? When you had your first heartbreak? When you were on autopilot? When you got a new job or lost your first job? When you started at a new school? When you had a baby or lost a baby? At what time did your inner bully start showing up? It is up to each of you to identify that moment. It will help you understand why you use to be a certain way. It will help you understand why you gave up certain things or allowed certain things to happen in your life. Find that moment, it will help you understand where you are in your life today. This will help you let go of the continuing harm you may be putting yourself through from that adjustment your inner bully set in your sail.

I have figured out when my inner bully was born. It took me a lot of reflection. As I reflected, I found myself working out some confusing moments in my past and I must share this with you.

I had feelings of sadness and insecurity that became stronger during my adolescence years, which was confusing because during that time I had some awesome things going on. I was a four-sport athlete. I made the varsity squad on every team I ever tried out for. I had a wonderful, steady boyfriend for a couple years during high school. I was senior class homecoming queen. I was getting decent grades and I'll bet my classmates would have said I was a happy, popular girl.

My greatest struggles began during my freshman year of high school. This is classically when the inner bully really embeds itself into your subconscious mind and plants itself there to remind you of all that is bad or at least all that can be perceived as being bad. My trigger began when a few upper classmen began constantly picking on me. I knew this was because they were jealous of me and felt threatened by the fact that I, a lowly freshman, was on a varsity team and present in their circle of friends and activities. Yet, even though I knew this on a rational level, I couldn't shake off the bad feelings I had. I also struggled because I was surrounded by upper classmen on these teams and I missed my old friends and teammates from junior high. *The change was difficult.*

The key word here is "change." It is important to recognize and remember that whenever there is change in your life, the inner bully is activated and stands ready to bring you down.

> *"Nobody on this earth can make you feel inferior,*
> *unless you give them permission."*
> –ZIG ZIGLAR

On top of the bullying I got from upperclassman, I experienced some pushback from some "friends" in my grade that would say things like, "Oh! You think you're too good for us now that you're on varsity!" The comments hurt. Suddenly, sports—the one thing I was good at and something that had brought me so much joy—was bringing me so much pain. I allowed the comments and bullying to get to me. I excluded myself by not letting anyone, truly, into my heart. Fortunately, I had one good friend that I felt didn't judge me and wasn't talking badly about me behind my back. Yet, unfortunately, by sixteen, I truly felt caught in the vortex of depression. My self-critiquing become more rampant. I never felt good enough. I felt utterly alone. How could this be?

Things changed little throughout the next decade of my life. At times, I experienced relative highs, but, on the whole, I still wasn't feeling fulfilled. It had little to do with a lack of worldly accomplishments. In fact, throughout that time, I was doing objectively very well. I had an education, a good job, a supportive family, and good friends. Yet, throughout my twenties, I continued to bully myself. I didn't know any better. I badgered my self-confidence and told myself that nothing I did was good enough, I didn't look good enough, or work well enough; I wasn't charming enough or smart enough. The list of my inadequacies went on and on in my head, dictated by my unrefined and merciless inner bully.

Before I had my "Aha!" moment at the age of thirty-one, I wondered if my depression stemmed from having been born the fourth of five children, or because I'd been bullied in my past, or if it was due to the fact that I'd been a tomboy rather than a traditionally pretty girl. If it wasn't because of any of these things, was it because I had something truly chemically wrong with me? Was it something beyond my self-control? I looked like I was happy and working properly, and that I had it all together on the outside, but for some reason I had something internal going wrong and it had been going wrong for a very long time. Was I a lemon?

*"We are products of our past, but we don't have
to be prisoners of it."*
–RICK WARREN

In reality, the bullies in high school were just the icing on the cake. My negative internal bully had embedded itself in my mind long before. What was truly causing this inner turmoil? Was it in my past or was it in me?

If it was my past, then the answer to what caused my inner bully to first emerge, which caused me such inner turmoil, can be linked to my second-grade teacher. I had trouble learning to read. I was eight years old when my teacher told me I would never amount to anything in life if I didn't learn to read better. This is a pretty harsh thing to say to an eight-year-old, but it gets worse. She said this in front of the whole class! I remember everyone staring at me as I sat there. She kept yelling at me and shaking a pointed finger at me from across the room. She had called on me to answer something about a story we'd read, on our own, during silent reading time and I told her I wasn't sure of the answer, because I didn't remember what I'd read. It wasn't that I didn't read the story; I didn't comprehend it. I struggled with comprehension. My mind would always wander. I'd be thinking of other things while I was reading and before I knew it I'd be one or two pages in and I'd have to start all over again, having forgotten what I'd just read. I felt so stupid! Did everyone in the class know the answer but me? She always gave me the skinny books while the other kids got the fat books, a constant reminder that I was somehow less than them and not good enough to get the cooler, newer, prettier, thicker books. I wasn't "smart" or "worthy" *or so that's what I thought*. Every time the word "read" or "reading" came up I would get sweaty and anxious. I just knew the only reason my teacher wanted to call on me was to make me feel bad. So, I wonder, was my experience in second grade the starting point for my eroded self-esteem that led to my spiraling depression? Did this lead to an adolescence and adulthood filled with feeling less-than?

After this experience in second grade, I started to act out. I'd try to get kicked out of class before it was reading time. If that failed, I'd try to speed read ahead of the rest of the class, making sure I knew the big words before

I was called on to read because when we had group-reading, we'd each take turns. I wanted to be sure to know all the words if I was called on, so I wouldn't mess up and empower the teacher to ridicule me in front of the class. This was a flawed plan, but when you're eight it seems like a really good plan. I continued doing this into high school. This pattern of behavior, stemming from anxiety, led me further and further behind in class. I finally developed a huge anxiety towards books, classroom group work, teachers, and ultimately, school. Something had to be wrong with me. I actually asked if I could be tested for special education classes because I thought I had a learning disability. I remember being brought in this tiny room where I would move blocks around and read little inserts. After every answer I gave, the monitor would write something down on a sheet of paper. I only hoped that as a result of these tests, someone would let me know what was wrong with me. Why couldn't I be as good as every other kid? I thought I was the only child with this problem. These tests never showed that I had any special problem, only that I was behind in just about every subject in the education program.

"What the teacher is, is more important than what he teaches."
–KARL MENNINGER

I'm sure most of you have experienced bullies in your lives like my second-grade teacher. We have all had good, bad, and ugly teachers. The gifted teachers inspire you. They make you feel so smart, so special, and so happy. When you have a teacher who believes in you, it's a lot easier to find purpose at school, so it's a lot easier to show up. All teachers should inspire their students and create a sense of safety and protection, physically and intellectually. The absence of this kind of security will cut deep into the hearts of children. A sense of inspiration and feeling of safety should come from all adults, regardless of their role in a child's life. Even if you were able to slither through school without a teacher like I had in second grade, I would bet you've still experienced bullies like her. Maybe, someone who put you down, hurt you, or caused you pain. Maybe a parent, an aunt or uncle, maybe even a stranger. Whomever you had to deal with in your past, I am sorry you had to go through that, but there are great lessons to be learned that will strengthen you and I am here to help you!

I have spent over ten years as a professional educator. My second-grade teacher may not have realized what damage she did to my young spirit, but she scarred me pretty badly. If I were in second grade, today, I would be diagnosed with ADHD and dyslexia. I'd be given wonderful, alternative assignments and teachers would use a variety of teaching strategies to help me learn. I finally got help in college where I was diagnosed with both ADHD and dyslexia and was finally taught strategies to help me with the challenges I faced. So, I wasn't stupid. I'm just a fixable lemon. Right?

As a child, we all have moments of feeling "less-than." Some of us can shrug them off and move forward while others, like myself, will search inside themselves for a deeper, "Why me?" meaning. It's amazing to me that there are people who go through life without feeling depressed. That may be wonderful for them, but as humans, we have a spectrum of thoughts and feelings and sometimes those thoughts or feelings may bring us down. So, even if you don't label yourself as a "depressed person" or say you've ever battled depression, there is still a bully in your life and you still have to deal with that bully; perhaps, you have mastered how to tame it.

We all have a bully in our lives. That's the reason I've written this book. There are two types of bullies that stalk you: *external bullies of your past and present* and your *internal bully*. External bullies come and go, like the upperclassmen of my past; but we can be victimized by the internal bully forever. With the knowledge gained from this book, you will be better able to repel *any* future bully you may come across but most importantly, once you learn to understand and recognize who and what your own lifetime internal bully is, how to identify it, and how to overcome it, you will thrive beyond what you've ever imagined.

Remember, the internal bully that victimizes you, sabotages your success and causes you to feel failure is YOU! Your inner bully is hungry and messes with your emotional state 24/7. Your inner bully will feed off of your issues, will feed off of change, will even feed off of hormonal imbalances. It will feed off both your sad times and your happy times. It will feed off your vulnerability in all stages of your life. You have all the control. *Don't let it feed off your insecurities and doubts!*

> *"Man's mind, once stretched by a new idea,*
> *never regains its original dimensions."*
> –OLIVER WENDELL HOLMES

Identify Your Life Steps & Patterns

You have all experienced bullies. You've either been a bully or you've been bullied. Most often, both have been the case! It's hard for kids to deal with external bullies and it doesn't get any easier for adults. We hear and see messages all over public schools about "bully awareness" and yet at those same schools there are parents, even teachers and staff that are bullies. It's silly to think adult bullies exist, like a contradiction in terms, and yet they do. The world is full of bullies, but when it comes to the toxic power over you, you can forget the external bullies. You need to get rid of the biggest bully in your life, and once you're able to defeat the biggest bully of all, you will be better resistant to external bullies.

You may be thinking, "I thought this book was about happiness and success." This book is about finding true happiness and success by becoming more *whole*. To become *whole*, you have to defeat the inner bully that lives in your mind.

It may be hard for an eight-year old or even a twelve-year old to understand that the bullies around them are nothing compared to the bully that lives within them, but we must all learn that we are only truly bullied when we bully ourselves. Once you grasp this concept and practice the ideas in this book to eliminate your true inner bully, you can then start helping your children and others around you to see that it is when they bully themselves that real destruction ensues. You need to realize that you are the one holding yourself back from true happiness and success. Remember, we are all involved in a dance every day of our lives. The steps we take can flow easily or be choppy and misguided causing us to stumble and trip over ourselves. We need to own our dance, find our balance, and smile joyously while we take each step. If you skipped the introduction, go back now and read it to understand that your life is a dance and that your inner bully would love nothing more than to cut in and lead your life's dance.

Okay, you know you are the real bully and you understand that you can become the biggest bully in your own life. You see that your inner bully is not there to help you succeed or improve, and yet you still entertain your inner bully when you need to be focusing on improving yourself. So, how do you improve yourself? And what is it about yourself that you need to improve? Here's the answer: You have to take a comprehensive, whole approach to self-improvement. *It is not only one thing you do but rather, a combination of little things you will do over time that will help improve your overall mindfulness and your life.* There is no quick fix. It does not come down to making adjustments in only one area of your life. All areas of your life matter and are interconnected, so it is a *whole* approach. The *whole* approach is an effective process that takes time.

> *"Put your heart, mind, and soul into even your smallest acts.*
> *This is the secret to success."*
> –SWAMI SIVANANDA

Worksheet #3—The Happy-Whole-You Matrix

This third worksheet is the Happy-Whole-You Matrix, which encourages you to take a comprehensive approach to improving your life. This Happy-Whole-You Matrix worksheet combines everything we've discussed. You can view this daily to remind yourself of what you, as a *whole* person need to bring into your life.

www.HappyWholeYou.com

Are You Emotionally Mature?

Before we go on, you need to know where you are in your life right now. Identifying your individual mental maturity and state of mind at this very moment is vital to self-improvement. *Think through this!* The degree of both mental and emotional maturity varies from person to person. The exercises in the pages to come will improve your personal understanding of you and your inner bully. You will find what makes you tick and what sets off your personal inner bully.

A side note: During my educational courses, I learned that when you enter adulthood, the reasoning and decision-making systems in the frontal lobe of the brain are fully developed. This allows you to reason more clearly and to make better decisions. You are now in a position to recognize the nonsense any past bully has said or done to you. My professor wanted our country's future educators to understand this fact, so that if we were teaching at a junior high or high school, we would be prepared to find students who may do something without knowing why they truly did it. The course also taught different teaching strategies to help kids with different needs based on various levels of emotional maturity.

Today, I understand that my second-grade teacher hadn't meant to be a bully; she simply lacked the proper tools, resources, and training to know how to teach a student with my issues. She just didn't know any better. But now I know better because I've matured and grown since then. I can move forward from that experience and throw the accompanying negativity out of my mind. Too bad I can't go back and explain to my eight-year-old-self what was going on.

The important thing is that I understand it now. I can tell myself it is okay and move on. I learned from this experience. I went through that difficult experience and, though I had struggles, hurt feelings, and unhealthy experiences, those experiences taught me to be a more compassionate and more understanding person. I am now thankful for the experience. I cannot change the way I felt in the past but I can change the way I feel and act moving forward. And even when the inner bully tries to use my past against me, I remind myself of the lesson learned.

I would like you to take a moment and describe a time in your life when you went through a difficult, hurtful experience at the hands of an external bully. Identify that experience and the profound impact it had on who you are today. You may have more than one experience (I think we all do), but let's start with the one that was a tipping or turning point that changed the direction of your life-dance. Include how that experience has positively impacted your current self. Write your answers below.

The turning point that changed your life's dance:

That experience positively impacted your present life:

> *"The only way that we can live is if we grow. The only way that we can grow is if we change. The only way that we can change is if we learn. The only way we can learn is if we are exposed. And the only way that we can become exposed is if we throw ourselves out into the open. Do it. Throw yourself."*
> –C. JOYBELL C.

Now that you understand that your frontal lobe is not fully developed in early adulthood, and you can make better sense of your childhood experiences, ask yourself if you have continued to allow a childhood or adolescent event to negatively impact your mental well-being. Have you allowed yourself to learn from that experience and throw the negativity away or have you held onto it and allowed your inner bully to beat you up with it?

I hope you're able to identify some positive outcomes that arose from an unfortunate, painful event, but is there a lingering residue still clogging up your mind from that event? *That's your inner bully!* Stop it! Chances are if you've come up with positive lessons learned from your past bully experience, that event is no longer bullying you. So, what is? What are you bullying yourself about right now?

You are, most likely, the hardest person on yourself. There is a certain drive, a certain push that makes us work harder. It is a healthy momentum that has the power to suppress the inner bully. It's called *action* and we will discuss it in depth later. But note, there is a significant difference between encouraging yourself to achieve and telling yourself you must achieve "or else."

Take a minute to think about how you could be bullying yourself. Write down three not-so-nice things you continuously do to yourself that make you feel bad and/or write down things you have done to sabotage yourself or sabotage an opportunity for yourself.

1.

2.

3.

Next, take a moment and write down three mechanisms that provide you with a positive push, three things that keep your inner bully at bay and allow you to flourish. I will share my three with you. The first is God and my family: my spouse, kids, mom, dad, and siblings. They are all positive drivers that encourage me to pursue my passions. Running is my second. Running provides me with the ability to clear my mind. It provides me with creative inspiration. My third positive push is my continuing education. The lessons learned from various books and trainings generate a deeper intellectual self-confidence. What are your three?

1.

2.

3.

Keep these three dream drivers at the forefront of your mind, always! Do not lose sight of these. Post these drivers somewhere that you can see them every day.

"Correction does much, but encouragement does more."
–JOHANN WOLFGANG VON GOETHE

Recognize Negative Self-Talk

If you are like most people, you probably say negative things to yourself every day without even realizing it. Why do we do this? As a woman, I know women are creatures that strive towards perfection. We self-critique regularly. Some of the best moms I know put themselves down, whereas I view them as rock stars. I asked a few of my rock star friends, "What are you most critical of when it comes to yourself? Here are their responses:

"Not being organized, stress eating, wrinkles, and dark circles."
MOM OF THREE, ages 7, 5, and 3, age 38, married;

"My self-worth; I compare myself to others and wonder why I can't be as good as them in life, like parenting, being a good wife, a good daughter."
MOM OF FOUR, ages 5, 10, 13, 15, age 37, married;

"I am not getting enough done."
MOM OF FIVE GROWN CHILDREN, age 60, married;

"How come I can't get my shit together? I can't seem to get organized at home."
MOM OF TWO, a 12-year-old, 18-year-old, and adopted 16-year-old, age 46, married;

"I feel I am not capable of doing what I am hired to do. It's too good to be true sometimes."
FEMALE, age 25, single;

"I feel guilty because I sometimes resent my children because I feel my husband and I have lost our marriage since having them."
MOM OF TWO, age 38, married;

"I am looking old these days."
MOM OF TWO ADULTS, age 64, divorced;

"Being-fat!"
MOM OF TWO, 1-year-old and 3-year-old, age 33, married;

"Losing my patience with my kids and comparing myself to others."
MOM OF TWINS, age 3.5, age 40, married.

I asked some of these women the question face-to-face while others I asked via text message. What I found interesting was that the individuals I asked in person were initially hesitant to answer. They seemed to go into deep thought then, when they would start to answer they would stop themselves and say things like, "I don't know," or, "There are so many." However, once they were no longer tongue-tied, they spilled out one critical thing about themselves after another. One friend said, "I have a lot more if you need it!" What's that all about? The inner bully was controlling their thoughts! I thought I might get more benevolent responses if I sent out the question as a text message, but I was wrong. I received honest, long text messages back, with multiple critiques. I chose to list the main critique from each participant's inner bully above.

One friend I surveyed had an inside scoop on what I was working on and the reason for my question. I sent her part of this book in its early stages, so when I received her message I knew I had to share the whole thing with you because she kept it real.

"This may sound weird but every day when I look in the mirror I critique my looks, hair, skin, belly pudge, clothes, but honestly as soon as I turn away, I am over it and don't give a shit any more. I am not big into mirrors or selfies but while I am looking, I always wish I could style my hair nicer or that my stomach was smaller. But then I tell my inner-bully to kiss my ass and I go on with my day, ha-ha! Looks obviously aren't at the top of my priority list but you should see the pictures of me in middle school. Talk about awkward!" Mom of two, ages 1 and 4, age 32, married.

I love how my friend moved away from her initial bully thoughts. She also shared with me that she is working on being nicer to herself. This is a perfect example of how we need to catch our bully moments and redirect them.

I also wanted to survey some of my male friends. All of these men were surveyed via text message. The men who responded (not all did) took a long time to respond compared to the women who took only minutes to reply. Maybe these men were in deep thought trying to find something to share, or perhaps men are not as self-critical as women, or maybe they were not comfortable sharing their self-criticism with me. Below are the text messages I received back from the male participants:

"Hmm"
DAD OF ONE, age 10, divorced, age 46;

"Impatient and not having enough time."
DAD OF FOUR, three adult children and one age 11, divorced, age 45;

"That I am selfish and my wife can do better than me."
DAD OF THREE, ages 16, 18, and 23, married, age 52;

"Poor self-body image."
DAD OF TWO, ages 1 and 4, married, age 35;

"I just don't like me sometimes."
DAD OF ONE, age six, married, age 39;

"I need to be lighter and quicker."
DAD OF ONE, age 11, married, age 42.

The responses from the men were neither as detailed nor were they multiple. However, more importantly for our purposes, there certainly does seem to be a negative voice present within the male mind as well.

We all need to be aware of the power of the destructive things we say to ourselves. Maybe you do what I do. When I'm getting dressed in the morning I find myself thinking things like, "I look tired today," or "This outfit makes my hips look big." or "What if I don't close that deal today?" or "I totally bonked at that presentation yesterday." This is not an encouraging way to begin the day.

The inner bully likes to use negative thoughts and anxiety to control you. You need to correct and block these low blows right away. These comments may seem to be small and unobtrusive but little by little, they dash your spirit. Ignorance is not bliss when it comes to subliminal, negative thoughts. Thoughts that sabotage you must be recognized right away. Some thoughts are so routinely told by your internal bully that you may have lost your ability to view them as what they are. But, in fact, the more habitual, the more destructive they are. These adverse thoughts show up and try to trip up your life's dance. Your internal bully can be telling you the same things over and over again, day-in and day-out and you start to believe and live under the rule of these negative thoughts. You need to realize it is up to you to stop this. Write down three negative things you've said to yourself today.

1.

2.

3.

Next, I want you to cross each negative thing out and tell yourself you are sorry you said that. Tell yourself that you didn't really mean each one. Then replace each negative thing on your list with a positive statement. Now, give yourself a hug! Seriously, visualize giving yourself a big warm hug and say, "I'm sorry!" *Be kind to yourself!*

Can you explain why you said these not-so-nice things to yourself? Why did you sabotage yourself like that? Why are you getting in your own way?

Why are you knocking yourself down when you are trying to dance? What is going on with you right now? Explain:

1.

2.

3.

Take a deep breath, relax, and hug yourself again. Now think of what you will do in the future instead of being a bully to yourself. What will you say or do in place of the three negative things you listed earlier above? This may seem like a silly thing to do, but you need to do it! Yes, you really need to do the *feel-good* stuff. You need to work on your *mindfulness*. What is it to be mindful? Simply put, it's being aware while using every one of your senses and your mind into whatever you're doing.

If your thoughts are not conducive to success, you will continually hold yourself back from your true potential. And remember, thinking good thoughts about yourself is a must to suppress your inner bully. It is not conceited or self-righteous; it is simply you being nice to you. If you said half the negative things you say to yourself to others, you would probably be considered a mean person. So be kind to yourself and list nice alternative thoughts and or actions you can do for yourself, every day, in place of the negative.

1.

2.

3.

Are you feeling any better? Are you still wondering why you're continuing to read this? Are you confused and feeling negative or skeptical about doing this work? If you are, it's your inner bully, fighting for its survival. Don't let your internal bully win. Don't let it stop you from enhancing your life and reaching your goals to be the best you possible. This takes time. Keep reading! During this process, you must approach yourself in a caring manner. You must set your goals higher than you ever before thought possible.

Practice what you learn in this book and your inner happiness will start to shine through and success will appear. Notice, I use the word "practice" because perfect, happy, *wholeness* is not something you can ever fully achieve because it is not static. You are not static and your life is not static, it is constantly moving. You are constantly moving. In your life's dance, you keep moving and making adjustments as you go; it never ends. Your life and therefore, your dance, will never be perfect. It's fluid and every step is interconnected with the steps before and the steps that come after. You must change what is going on within you before things will change around you. You cannot stay the same and expect things around you to be any different. Stay with me a bit longer and I just know you will feel more *whole*, freer, and more on track to find true happiness and success.

> *"Have no fear of perfection. You'll never reach it."*
> –SALVADOR DALI

Identify Your Issues

Everyone has issues. Learning to recognize your issues is very valuable. Whether the issue is: being habitually late, choosing unhealthy relationships, constantly interrupting people, over spending, putting people down, not knowing when to stop—you get the idea. These issues amount to the greater portion of your inner bully's script and you are better than these issues. For example: If you have the issue of saying, sorry for everything—sorry I can't make it, or sorry I will look into that—you should try saying, "I would love to attend, but I am unavailable," and "Thank you, I will look into that." Another example is when you are home, cleaning and cooking, taking care of children and your spouse comes home and says, "Dinner isn't ready?" When your first response is, "Sorry, I have been cleaning and taking care of the kids." Stop yourself right there! Your response should be, "Not yet, but it will be ready soon and I could use your help!" Stop putting sorry in front of every sentence and put a positive spin on your response.

If you are emotionally mature, you've learned to separate your issues from yourself as you acknowledge all you have to be grateful for. You can distinguish between who you are as a total person and your individual issues. They don't *become* you and take over your life or jaundice your view of life. The healthy, emotionally mature you, acknowledges them and learns to deal with and grow from them.

When you distinguish between your issues and your total-self, those issues will no longer set you in a downward spiral that saps your strength. You can deal more effectively with resolving them and evolve past them because you are in control and your perspective is clear. When you separate yourself from the issue you are no longer playing the blame game. You are not blaming yourself or anyone else. When you accept the issue, be it money problems, weight gain, loss of a loved one, or anything else, you can move forward and grow. You can focus on your goals, with strength. That is a great place to be. You can't get there if you are wallowing in the issue. Allow yourself time to come out on top of an issue. It takes practice. Your emotional maturity will grow as you work through this book.

> *"If you choose to not deal with an issue, then you give up*
> *your right of control over the issue and it will select the path*
> *of least resistance."*
> –SUSAN DEL GATTO

You must get out there and take action against your inner bully. No longer will you let yourself feel "less-than" because of your issues; instead of allowing yourself to "feel less-than," you will find solutions. There is always a positive solution to any negative issue that your inner bully presents you with. *Always go to the positive!*

Take some time and write your past in a few paragraphs. Include the main events that you feel defined your current state of mind or a state of mind that controlled you for a period of time. What were some of your issues? What issues did you allow to have control over you?

What is your past story? Write it below:

_____

_____

_____

_____

_____

_____

_____

"Live life to the fullest, and focus on the positive."
–MATT CAM

Are You a "Yes" Person?

As you start to wrap your head around the idea that you are the real bully in your life and that the way you think is at the root of all your problems, it is important to think back through the chapters of your life. Think back through the times you can identify as having bullied yourself, instances when you sabotaged your own life. Remember, when bad things happen, we have a choice of how we are going to respond. You cannot blame others for your bully moments. By identifying how you are self-sabotaging, you'll be able to identify your existing patterns and see the truth in what I'm sharing with you. Again, these are things *you* did, not anyone else or something else, so own it, learn from it, and move forward. Remember, when you encounter someone who doesn't do what you'd like or things don't go your way, it is how you choose to respond that truly matters. It's time to *think* so you respond rather than react.

We've learned that the bully in you can be sneaky. You may not even realize it has cut into your life, especially if you are a do-gooder, a "yes" person, who puts everyone before yourself. If you are the "yes" person, STOP! I've met these people and re-trained them. I've been one of these people myself. "Yes" people don't take care of themselves as they should, and they use the excuse that they don't have time because they're too busy doing everything for everyone else. These people allow everyone else to lead their life's dance. They seem highly stressed, and usually appear to be super busy, but yet, they always make time to please everyone around them with a tiring charm and they will never say no. Do you know someone like this? Is this you?

Are you a "yes" person? If you are, it is my belief that your internal bully is making you feel that you have to do everything for everyone else, because you are not good enough to put yourself first or you do not want to deal with your issues, so you put all your focus on others. Of course, I'm not suggesting that doing things for others is a bad thing. It has actually been shown that helping others improves one's happiness; but when pleasing others consumes your life and disrupts your ability to properly nurture yourself, it is a very bad thing. There is a fine line between helping others and letting helping others control you.

If you are always doing for others in a way that never benefits you, it is doubtlessly causing you more stress than happiness. You are bullying yourself! Helping others should leave you feeling satisfied, not empty or asking what else you can do because you feel guilty for not doing enough. If you are left with displeasure after helping someone, you need to reflect. Everything can be made into a win-win situation. You might think it is selfish to think this way, but guess what? Happy, successful, *wholistic* people don't simply give away their time, money, or energy without receiving a positive benefit. The positive benefit can be a sense of peace you feel after helping or a sense of accomplishment for helping. It can also be because you helped someone with something, now they will be helping you. Life and all relationships should be a process of give and take. Yes, sometimes you may give more but you must develop win-win relationships. It's unhealthy if you're always doing for others and in return you are left feeling down and depressed, and wondering why no one is helping you. If this happens, it is because you set yourself up for that. You were helping the wrong people or saying yes to all the wrong things. When you decide to approach life in a way that you are always giving and pleasing others at the expense of your own well-being, you will find yourself empty. You can give, give, give, but at some point, you need to receive. You must be replenished.

Over the years, I have had the pleasure of personally training individuals that are "yes" people and I've always found it frustrating that these people tend to get in their own way of success. More, they believe that by continually saying "yes" and giving up everything for others will eventually make them happier. They're providing a service to others without being replenished. At the end of the day, if you can't support yourself emotionally, mentally, physically, and financially you're running very low on fuel, and it will show in all aspects of your life, and the burden then falls on us all! A win-win relationship can be volunteering at a school because you love to be around children, but volunteering at a school when you don't have the time and the kids cause you stress is not the right fit, even though you love kids. Another win-win relationship can be helping carpool with a friend but it is only carpooling if they help transport your kids as well. I have a friend whom I carpool with quite often. She has two kids in school, as do I. This makes for an easy carpool. I drop the kids off at school she picks them up. It is great! She has recently agreed to help another parent out with carpooling, which is fine; however, this third parent is not living up to they're part in the carpooling agreement and this has caused my friend stress. This disrupts her daily schedule, affecting her own children's after school snack and homework routine. Were this to happen once or twice it would be no biggie. But my friend has allowed this to continue for a while now and I have seen the stress it has caused her. This is not a win-win relationship.

Replace this carpooling example with something else. If you are in a relationship that started out as a win-win relationship but quickly turned into something causing you stress and dissatisfaction, it is up to you to stop it. Don't complain about it to others or let it stew inside of you. Speak to the person who is causing you this stress and let them know how you feel. Have a conversation using "I" statements. For example, you might say something like, "Sheri, I appreciate your willingness to try and carpool with us but I feel like I have been doing most of the carpooling lately. Is something going on?" See what Sheri has to say. Once Sheri has finished speaking (without interruption) decide what you want to do, based on that. What is best for you and your family? If you chose to not have the conversation, then you are choosing to add stress in your life and you do not have the right to be upset at or blame Sheri.

Another example of a win-win relationship can be swapping trade work. Say you have a plumbing business and your friend has a trailer business and you need some trailer work done and your buddy needs some plumbing done. Trade the work, but, most importantly, if you find it is becoming more than what you expected, you must have that conversation with your buddy and adjust the agreement accordingly.

A "yes" person will not have the important conversations and are left feeling cheated because they did way more than they got in return. Do not set yourself up for this. Talk it out.

Additionally, it's important to understand that by doing too much for others, we enable them and stunt their growth. Many parents are guilty of this with their children. They do everything for them and the child becomes too dependent on them later in life.

Take some time and reflect on your relationships to see if you can improve any of them. Remember, God gave you—*You first*! Take care of you, so you have the fuel to care for and do good things for others.

> *"If you always put someone else first, there's a tendency*
> *for others to depreciate you, to lose respect, because respect comes*
> *from an understanding that that person has her own wishes,*
> *dreams, and desires,"*
> –ETHEL S. PERSON, MD

Accepting Help

On the flip side of being someone who does everything for everyone else there is the "denier." The "denier" does not accept help from others. Do you turn down others who offer you help? Why? What is that about? I use to pass up offers of help. I thought I could just do everything all on my own; my inner bully told me it would be "easier." Why would I pass up help from others? To make things harder on myself! That's why! I was bullying myself thinking I had to do everything all on my own. I would tell myself no one could do a given thing as well as I could, or that it would just be easier to do things on my own. But the truth is, things are a lot more fun and more satisfying when you share the experience with others. Two is better than one and three is better than two! And so much more can get done! Learn to let others help you in all aspects of your life. This makes life more enjoyable and helps put your inner bully in check.

I know that sometimes, help from others can end up making more work for you and that's the kind of help you do not want, but please realize others can help you achieve your goals a lot sooner than doing it alone. You never know what someone else can teach you.

Think back to times in your life when others offered to help you. Did you let them? I'll bet some of those times when others offered you help, you were feeling overwhelmed and really needed the help but didn't take it, only to find yourself frustrated, stressed out, and overwhelmed. Right? Write out three times in your life that you denied help from others or didn't ask for help from others even though you really could have used it. If you cannot think of a time when this has happened, because you truly believe you never really need help from others you need to take a deeper look. Surely, we all can use a little help at some point! Even if you truly believed you didn't need their help, would it be so bad to give someone else the satisfaction of believing they were helpful? And isn't it possible that you could learn something from the experience? Consistently denying help from others can be a bully moment and can lead to feelings of emptiness, selfishness, and frustration. List three instances when you denied help from others or didn't ask for help from others when the outcome would have been better with two people (or more) vs. you alone:

1.

2.

3.

Okay, now that you understand that you need to utilize helping hands and you don't need to do everything on your own, identify other ways and instances in which you allow your inner bully to cut into your life. Remember, one of the keys to ending personal bullying and creating *wholism* is to be able to recognize your bully moments. You must identify unconscious behavior patterns in your daily life. You must recognize habits that handicap you from true happiness and success. Remember working through these exercises is a way to allow you to grow and move forward.

> *"We are all here on earth to help each other;*
> *what others are here for I don't know!"*
> –W.H. AUDEN

Don't Play the Victim-
Own Your Life

My Depressed Dance

Why is it important to reflect on your past bully moments? As I shared with you earlier, I struggled with not feeling good enough, feeling less-than, and depressed for many years. I used to call this yucky feeling all sorts of different things depending on my stage in life. A person that sufferers from depression can find themselves asking "why me?" or blaming others for how they are feeling, and where they are in their life. I used to think that my depression was rooted in my childhood, or was it because I wasn't good enough, or because I felt like a tomboy, or because I felt I didn't get enough one-on-one attention, or because I wasn't the "pretty" sister, or because I was bullied, or poor, or stupid, or didn't have enough true friends? I could go on and on. We all have our stories of struggles and daily challenges; that's life. But there's also the silver lining we must find. We have to go through the bad to appreciate, to see, and to learn what is good. We sometimes have to lose to win.

I remember when I took my first job after college. Since I couldn't find a job I wanted in Michigan, where I grew up, I thought I'd move out of state and life would be great. Before I took that job, I looked into other opportunities in both Florida and New York, but neither of those states matched what I was looking for, so I took a job in California. I flew out to Bakersfield, California to check out the scenery. I remember it was a clear, sunny April day and you could see the beautiful mountains off in the distance. There was a nice breeze and the people were very friendly. To top it off, I was offered $2,400 as a moving bonus, so as a twenty-two-year-old, broke, college graduate it seemed like the deal of a lifetime. I was all in.

A couple months later, I asked my sister and my best friend, to join me on a road trip to California. I stuffed my green Lumina with all my clothes, a few pots and pans, and we were on our way. I was excited about starting my new life. I actually remember thinking how happy I was going to be. "Now I'll be happy, because I'll be in California making $42,000 a year, and I'll be able to reinvent myself." It was wrong to think that moving across the country and having some money would make me truly happy. My way of thinking was screwy. *Why the heck did I feel I needed to reinvent myself anyway?* Because when you're always bullying yourself you believe that your current self isn't good enough. You begin to believe that everything outside of you holds the key to your happiness. The inner bully thrives on making you believe this. Do not ever think you have to reinvent yourself! Instead, think you need to add more value and knowledge to yourself. Think of enhancing your life. We all have everything to be happy within us; it just comes down to allowing yourself to utilize your inner resources, in the right way. When you learn to do this, success will follow.

There was no need for me to reinvent myself. Months before I moved to California, I had graduated from Western Michigan University (GO BRONCOS!). I consistently took between 14 and 19 semester credits and enrolled in summer courses. As a result, I was able to finish all my studies in 3.5 years, after which I immediately started a semester internship. This was an outstanding achievement, considering that the program took many students five years to complete. While in college, I also worked as a fitness instructor and trainer and, in addition, ran for the university's cross-country and track team. (I didn't perform well as a runner in college because I didn't allow myself to be good. I will discuss this aspect in greater depth later.)

Furthermore, upon graduating, I was only $16,000 in debt, which was also amazing, as I'd funded my entire college education through my own hard work, a few small scholarships, and a few thousand dollars I received from my parents. I was already a go-getter, self-sufficient, and successful. So again, why was it that after graduation I thought I had to reinvent myself? Because my inner bully was leading my life!

In college, my inner bully screwed with my mind even more so than in high school. Thankfully I didn't have any external bullies to deal with in college (which is probably one of the best things about college). There were no more cliques, and being different in college is welcomed! I only had my internal bully to deal with. I remember thinking I was never going to finish college. A part of me was always waiting for that one class I wouldn't pass, that one class that would hold me back from getting my degree. My inner bully used this fear to fuel my self-doubt. My second-grade teacher's voice never left my head. I allowed myself to use her negative words as my own. I allowed those words to push me down and feed my inner bully. Thankfully, I was both stronger and smarter than she or I had realized, and I never, in fact, failed a class. I was way smarter than I thought.

Despite all the successful endeavors I had, I didn't feel truly successful. I continued to let my inner bully put me down and control my thoughts. It was these negative self-talks that led me to believe I needed to reinvent myself in California.

Remember, if you allow yourself to hold on to the negative words or actions others direct at you, you will turn that negativity inward, into your own words and actions. Those who've been negative towards you or have wronged you in your past have moved on; so should you! Let go of the negativity! The best way to let go of the negative words others put in your mind is to continue to improve yourself, just as you are reading this book to improve yourself, these questions and exercises are helping you build a greater foundation for yourself. Keep building the good to let go of the bad.

When you fill your brain with many negative thoughts, your entire reality becomes consumed with negativity and consequently, your every outcome is viewed as negative. Unfortunately, I was so busy bullying myself during my college days that my negative reality never allowed me to enjoy life, nor to appreciate what a great job I was doing. Do you do this to yourself? Have you been doing something well, working hard, only to have some nagging thing in the back of your mind tell you that you are still not good enough or that what you're doing is still not great? That things will end badly for you and you'll end up failing? If this is you, *STOP!* You are a lot smarter and more talented than you give yourself credit for and you need to stop allowing the internal bully to overshadow your current successes with self-disapproving thoughts.

> *"Strength and growth come only through*
> *continuous effort and struggle."*
> –NAPOLEON HILL

Unfortunately, when all you think about is the negative that is all you will remember. Thinking back on my college years, the main things that stick out are recollections that I believed I was too fat to run well, I felt rushed and stressed-out 24/7. I didn't think I was pretty, and I felt impoverished. I was simply allowing the inner bully to feed me with these negative thoughts and in return I didn't take good care of myself. I'd party (to "feel more popular"), eat junk food, deprive myself of sleep, and then expected my body to run, function well, feel happy, and not feel stressed. *I don't think so!* I chose to be unhealthy and allowed each of the poor choices I made to add weight to my life and this slowed my ability to run well.

Throughout college, I thought I was too busy to stop and take a moment to pat myself on the back and tell myself everything was going well. I was either rushing to complete an assignment, a workout, or a shift. I allowed stress to consume me. Do you do this? Are you rushing through life fully stressed out?

Thankfully, I can pat myself on the back now, and that's a strong, healthy place to be in life. You will get there too. But I sometimes wonder how many more joyous and wonderful memories I would have had of those weighed-down, stressful, depressed years if I could go back in time and show myself the love I deserved. To tell myself everything is all right and I was doing just fine—enjoy the moments. This is the lesson I have to accept from my past as I move on. When you don't take care of yourself you will miss out on some cool stuff.

"Be happy for this moment. This moment is your life."
                                                    –OMAR KHAYYAM

Slow Down to Go Fast

Many times, in life, we need to momentarily slowdown in order to gather ourselves, take a breath and continue to move forward. This is called "slowing down to go fast." When you draw all your energy and time focusing on what you need to do next, what you are lacking, and what you are stressed about (examples of going too fast) you lose the ability to enjoy the moments that make up your life. You miss opportunities to congratulate yourself on how well you're doing and how blessed you are. You forget that the little things make up the big things. You need to slow down to see clearly and then you can move fast! When you're too focused on the outcome, too busy rushing to what is next (as I was), too busy creating stress in your life, you steal your ability to enjoy the process and you can lose sight of the good that is happening.

I must share a problem that I had. My memory was very poor. From the ages of about 16-26 or so, I had a lot of blank years in my mind. I couldn't remember a lot of events my friends spoke of. I asked my doctor about this and after running some test, he shared with me that my stress hormone, cortisol, was very high and that causes a lack of memory. So not only was the stress of rushing to what was next taking away my ability to enjoy the little things, my stress had provided me the inability to even remember some of my history.

As I labeled this section, *slow down to go fast*, I want you to remind yourself of this. We need to take in the moments, pat ourselves on the back, and not worry. We need to let go of the stress or we end up letting go of memories.

Do you focus on things that are out of your control and allow them to consume you and negatively impact your well-being? I have. I remember feeling not good enough, feeling less-than every other girl in college because guys didn't ask me out. Yes, I actually let this dramatically impact my self-esteem and my concept of self-worth. No one had told me that I shouldn't take it personally. College may not be the best place for dating. I want to share that with you! If *you* met your lifelong love in college, that is awesome, but I think the majority of college students will study, go out to have a good time, play the field, and look towards their future career. I also recall that lots of students went on trips for spring break and I felt bad because I couldn't afford to go anywhere. Again, focusing on something that was out of my control and obviously had nothing to do with me or with my self-worth; however, it didn't stop my inner bully from using that as bait. I didn't know then that many of the other college kids were only able to go on spring break trips because they used credit cards (more on the use of credit later) or their parents were paying their way. Let's be honest: spring break is not a spa retreat; it relaxes neither your body nor your mind. I'd guess those who've taken trips on their college spring break, usually feel the need to recover for a few days when they return. Why did I focus on these things that were out of my control? What do you focus on that is out of your control?

Remember, enjoy the process of your life evolving, stop comparing yourself to others, and enjoy the little moments. The reality is you only have the present moment, so, slow down, pat yourself on the back, breath, listen to your life song, and dance!

> *"God, grant me the serenity to accept the things I cannot change,*
> *The courage to change the things I can,*
> *And the wisdom to know the difference."*
> −REINHOLD NIEBUHR

Poor Me!

During the ages of eighteen to twenty-two, I thought, *"Poor me... Poor me... Poor me,"* all too often. *LAME!* I honestly thought everyone else had it all together and enough money to do what they wanted. I even though everyone else had a date on Friday and Saturday night! Wow, was I wrong to think this way! To think that everyone else's life was perfect. But even if I wasn't wrong and their lives were more perfect than mine, what does someone else's choices and opportunities have to do with me? Do you focus on what others do and what they have? Why should any of us feel the need to compare ourselves with others? *We shouldn't!* Comparing yourself to others, just to focus on what they have and what you don't have, is a scene directed by your inner bully!

A side note for all of you dealing with social media: I'm thankful that during my time in high school and college I didn't have to deal with Facebook, Snapchat, Instagram, and the host of other social media platforms that would have, no doubt, really messed up my head even more. Social media can be incredibly misleading. If you already have insecurities, self-doubt, and compare yourself to others, stay clear of social media; at the very least, really limit your exposure. If you are deeply into social media—even if you use it sparingly—take a social media detox. Stay off of all social media for seven days; then, on day six or seven, evaluate how you're feeling. Any better? Remember, what you see on social media is not as real as you might think. If you think it's real, I would suggest you take a second look. Social media, to me, is as real as reality shows. Reality shows tend to be "set-up," scripted and far from real. First come all the "set-up" shots and suggested scripts, then all the many, many edits and filters, until what you're left with is at most a fraction of the truth. Likewise, on social media, you are only seeing what others want you to see. It is a snapshot of a much bigger picture. I believe social media feeds your inner bully. Until you can fully practice a *wholistic* life, be confident in yourself, and appreciate yourself, you are not ready to expose yourself to social media in large doses. It can be the madness that sends you flying over the edge. Eliminating social media for a period of time could bring on the turning point you are working towards.

You are an easy target when you feed your inner bully with social media, negative thoughts, comparing yourself to others, and beat yourself down. Unfortunately, you can never get away from your inner bully. It is always there. You can only change how effectively you deal with your inner bully through learning and growth. Your inner bully, perhaps fueled by social media, will encourage you to have a "poor-me" attitude. Having a "poor-me" attitude never serves you well. It will always make you feel like a victim, depressed and "less-than."

The inner bully of my college days was still dominating me when I made the move to California and by this time social media was polluting my mind. My short window of hope, when I started my new life, was quickly interrupted with my "poor-me" attitude and reminders from my inner bully; I listened to it and believed it. It only took me a few months, set in my new life, having received multiple paychecks and having lost weight, to admit I was still not happy. What the heck! How could that be? I finally had money, I'd lost weight, and I had a good job. I even had dates and there were no more college papers to write. Now what was my problem? The self-bullying continued mercilessly. The cycle I've described is vicious and the small poor choices I was making were weighing me down once again, bit by bit, ten weighted pounds at a time. The distraction of the new scenery and new job was only that, a distraction.

After three unhappy years at my new job in California with an ever-increasing paycheck in sharp contrast to my steadily decreasing happiness, I decided I was "so depressed" that I needed to see a psychiatrist. Yup, once again, I went searching for something external to fix me. I still hadn't figured out that I needed to improve myself. I hadn't yet learned that I held the key to unlock my happiness and that only I could rid myself of my depression.

I decided that a doctor would unlock the door to my happiness. My family doctor put me on Prozac. Unfortunately, that didn't work, so of course, I thought I needed a different doctor. I figured since the new job, higher pay, and weight loss did not work, a new pill and new doctor had to be the answer. I needed a psychiatrist! *Yes, that had to be the solution, right? Nope!* I was wrong again! My psychiatrist had me on three different medications. Triple the happiness, right? *Wrong!*

The psychiatrist had me coming for office visits every couple of months without showing any progress, he kept the same routine at each visit. All sessions started with a series of questions that sounded something like, "Do you want to kill yourself? Do you want to hurt others? Do you hear or see spirits?" He actually made me feel as though I was truly crazy. At the end of each session he would hand me three prescriptions and I would be on my way. He never truly spoke to me. It was always so scripted. He was more of a pill pusher; get me in and get me out.

The doctor said, "Yes, you are depressed and need to be medicated," and so naturally, that became my reality, my new label. I was a depressed person who needed help from a medical professional and pills. I know now that this was crazy thinking. Just because someone with a white coat and a plaque on the wall told me something, I naturally accepted everything he said and prescribed to me without questioning him (but not for long). Neither the medical professional nor the pills would help me, but I didn't know it at the time. I still had some learning to do, so in the "meantime," like clockwork, I came and went to my visits.

In truth, I was convincing myself that I was very depressed. I'd given someone else control over my feelings as if they were not for me to control, "Poor-me!" Of course, I was the one who always had all the control. I just didn't know it.

You have all the control with your well-being. No one has greater control over you than you. This is sometimes hard to see when you are in the thick of the dance with your inner bully, leading you, pulling you, twirling you, and throwing you around so quickly you can't see what's coming next. When this starts to happen, you must buckle down and say, "STOP!" Take a deep breath, look around, and remind yourself that you, and only you, have all the control.

My time to yell, "STOP!" was coming close. After many, many months of seeing my psychiatrist, and not feeling any better, I was getting sick of still being sad and depressed. I still felt no improvement though I was taking all the pills he'd prescribed and I was showing up for all my visits! For many of you who have been in the thick of it with your inner bully—in the deep yuck drowning, in what feels like, thick black oil suffocating you—you will reach a breaking point when you either give in to your inner bully or you pull yourself up and start to move towards the light. Remember, always go towards the light and the dark shadows will stay behind you!

I almost let the inner bully not only win, but also completely destroy me during that period of time. I remember very clearly when I felt like I had hit rock bottom. I felt so horrible, so hurt, and so bad inside I was almost numb. I was ready to either kill myself or leave everything behind and disappear. Pack my stuff up, quit my job, and try to find my way back to Michigan.

Thank goodness when I hit this bottom feeling, my mom was visiting for a holiday break. I admitted to her the sad fact that I no longer wanted to be alive. I'd find myself daydreaming about being dead and assumed no one would really miss me. My mom suggested we go to a psych ward. We actually did go to one and we asked what kind of help I would get if I were to admit myself. The lady explained that there would be one-on-one sessions with a psychiatrist as well as group sessions. My mom asked what type of activities they had for patients. "What do you mean?" asked the woman, confused. My mom said, "Well, if my daughter won't be able to be active, and do some activities she'll only get worse." My mom was right! Exercise and physical activity had always been the one thing that helped me clear my mind and had prevented me from going over the edge. This ward had a reductionist approach. They would have me see a doctor and prescribe me medication. The food there was not healthy and you would be stuck inside 24/7. I did not enter the ward that day. When we left, I felt so tired, so empty, so sad. I was sick of feeling so bad and searching for an answer. I knew that killing myself would truly be an act of extreme selfishness and I just couldn't do that to my family, so I told my mom I was just going to quit my job and move back home. She warned me that I would be leaving a good job and that moving back home would not change how I was feeling. She was right. Again, I was searching for something outside of myself to fix myself. She reminded me I had so much more to live for.

I went back to my psychiatrist shortly after my mom returned to Michigan. For once I was actually looking forward to my visit with him. I planned to tell him he was not helping me and that the pills were not helping me. I wanted to ask him for a new regimen. What I got was way better!

On the day of my appointment, I was optimistic that the psychiatrist would have another plan. After all, there had to be something else out there to rescue me. I wanted to get better. I was sick of being sick and being the victim of my own distress. Something deep inside of me was trying to shine light in my life.

As I was sitting in the ugly, depressing waiting room, with tan-colored walls that seemed to be closing in on me, I started to get annoyed. I looked around at the people sitting hunched over with their heads down as if ashamed they were there. I remember thinking that something was wrong with this picture. I registered more sadness than depression and I was angry. I felt like I was needlessly carrying a few hundred pounds on my shoulders and that weight was suffocating me. I felt heavier than ever. What was I doing? I felt I didn't belong there and the longer I waited for the doctor, the stronger the feeling grew. He was running late; twenty minutes, twenty-five, thirty minutes ticked by and the walls kept moving steadily towards me, pushing in closer and closer. I was growing more and more agitated and worked up. Then I became pissed off! I thought, all these "depressed" mentally unwell people are gathered here, waiting to be seen in this horribly depressing waiting room, listening to all the negative things that are going on in the world from a news station playing on the TV. My appointment time had passed 30 minutes ago, but no one let me know why the doctor was running late, or apologized, or gave me an idea of how much longer I'd have to wait. What the heck? Why did I have to wait so long? Doesn't the psychiatrist know I'm "crazy" and that he shouldn't leave a bunch of "crazy" people waiting in a small, gloomy room for long?

When my name was finally called, I walked quietly into the doctor's office and sat down on the brown leather couch as I'd I done many times before. This time, however, I was aggravated. The doctor never even looked at me (why didn't this bother me before?). He had his head down over my file and began spouting off the usual questions. Did I want to hurt or kill myself? Did I want to hurt others? Then we were interrupted by a call on his cell phone. Without saying "excuse me" and having still not looked at me, he answered his call. What? Was he kidding me? I was royally ticked off! He sat there talking on his phone for about 5 minutes, which is forever when you're sitting in the crazy person's doctor's office as upset as I was. When he hung up, he looked right back down at my file and continued his questions, still not even glancing at me, as if no phone call had ever taken place. He didn't skip a beat. "Do you see or hear spirits?" I had to stop him—and I did! I told him I didn't appreciate the fact that he'd answered his phone in session; it was rude and disrespectful. I told him that I had waited well over thirty minutes for my appointment and felt it was unjust for him to take a personal call during my appointment time, time I was paying for! He gave me a blank stare and said simply, "I had to take that call."

"Well," I said, "You could have at least excused yourself or said you were sorry. You could have acknowledged me."

"I am sorry," he replied.

It was an empty, awkward, "sorry" as if he wasn't sorry at all. What a quack!

The real sorry needed to come from me, a deep meaningful sorry to myself. In that next minute, I got up off that brown leather couch and told him I was leaving. He looked at me, confused, but as though he didn't really care. He handed me my three prescriptions and said, "I need to see you in a couple months."

I looked him in the eye and replied, "No, you don't!"

I never felt more powerful. Please understand, I did not yell at him. I was calm and added only a flare of mean girl in the tone of my voice. I was somewhat in shock that I had the strength to stand up for myself and that this doctor didn't care at all about me. What was I thinking? What had made me go to someone like him? I allowed him to treat me with a reductionist approach. I walked out of that doctor's office a changed woman. I told myself that I needed to take control of my life. I needed to take ownership of how I felt. I didn't refill my prescriptions and decided to start nurturing my inner-self instead. It was up to me to change the way I was feeling. Never again would I let someone or something take ownership of how I felt. I forgave myself.

After that appointment, I knew I'd have ups and downs, but, most importantly, I now knew I had control of how high my highs would go, and how often and how low I'd experience my lows. It is inevitable that there will be ups and downs in your life, but how you choose to feel about those ups and downs is up to you. Have you ever allowed someone else or something else to have control over how you were feeling? How did you get through it? Is it happening right now? How does this make you feel?

> *"Believe that life is worth living and your belief*
> *will help create that fact."*
> –WILLIAM JAMES

Be Determined

Find Purpose

We must all find our purpose and I knew I had to find mine. Do you sometimes have ups and downs that make or break your spirit? You can end the cycle of having too many downs and instead, increase your ups by finding purpose. As you have learned, it is your inner bully that takes you on this rollercoaster ride of ups and downs. There are various facets involved in defeating your inner bully and creating a happier ride on this rollercoaster of life. I want you to come out on top, living a *wholistic,* happy life.

A big part in defeating your inner bully is to identify your *"why."* *Why* do you want to get rid of the inner bully? *Why* do you want to improve your life? My *"why"* was that I no longer wanted to feel horrible! I no longer wanted to feel like a victim of my own self. I wanted to feel like I had control in my life. I wanted to feel happiness. I wanted to live a successful life, not a "poor-me" life. I wanted to have the control. I wanted to be in charge. You must know *your "why"* or you will never be able to change. Why do you want to change?

Your *why* should make you emotional when you talk about it. You have to be passionate about your *why*. Face it: The truth is you either want to change or you want to stay the same. Know *why* you want to grow and evolve, and accomplish greatness for yourself. Your *why,* if strong enough, will keep you pushing towards your ultimate dream! The inner bully cannot survive in someone who's always pushing towards their ultimate dream or *purpose* because it's when you're pushing towards your ultimate dream that you find strength and purpose. *Why* do you want what you want? What is your motivation, your *purpose*? If you can't yet verbalize your *purpose*, you will. First, just know *why* you want to change. You first have to know your *why* before your *purpose* will be revealed. Your *purpose* becomes the antidote that will defeat your inner bully when it shows up and tries to call the shots.

Once I used my *why* as fuel for personal change, I found my purpose. My purpose is to help as many people as I can to defeat their inner bully. I don't want you to feel what I have felt. I want you to live a *wholistic* life and feel the joys of all that is good. I found my *purpose* only when I decided to repeat *why* I wanted to change, over and over. My *why* and my *purpose* continue to grow greater, even today, as I continue to grow, and so will yours.

You need a strong *why* so that when things get hard and you feel another ten-pound weight thrown at you, you will be strong enough to throw that weight back. You can always shrug that weight off when you are living a purpose-driven life. Prepare yourself to be strong! Don't allow yourself to be knocked out, flattened and defeated before you even give yourself a chance to begin. Remember, this process takes time. Be patient with yourself. When the internal bully comes at you, your *why* needs to be so strong that your *purpose* comes to your aid, so that you become resistant to the negative pull of your inner bully. It is when you resist the inner bully that you are able to find clarity and you bless yourself with more inner strength and self-confidence.

You can't have a truly fulfilling life without having *all* aspects of your life working in harmony. To achieve that harmony, you need to make changes in your life. Now you know a large step towards success is to identify your "*why*." Give a detailed summary of *why* you are changing below. Take your time with this exercise. Slow down, close your eyes and take a couple deep breaths. Clear your mind and begin to write from your heart.

Why I am changing:

> *"When you walk in purpose, you collide with destiny."*
> –RALPH BUCHANAN

Reprogram Your Life

Now that you have your *why* written out, you are well on your way to finding your *purpose*. To reach your *purpose* you need to immerse yourself, dive into the second instrumental process, which will transform you. You must **reprogram your brain** to change your life. Yes, that's right, you need to change the way you think. This is a process that requires you to make little mental adjustments over time so that you will ultimately achieve a *whole* mindset.

Reprogramming my brain took time, but once I mastered this aspect of the new, *wholistic* me, I experienced feeling energized, happy, successful, and I danced with purpose. You will soon dance with your purpose!

> *"Folks are usually about as happy as they make their*
> *minds up to be. Make your purpose deciding to find success*
> *and true happiness in life."*
> –ABRAHAM LINCOLN

Reprogramming your brain will forever be a work in progress. It never ends; another way of saying this is that when you master this, you will continue to improve over time. I have been working hard over the last few years to reprogram my brain. Some positive shifts I've made in the way I think about myself and my life are: How wonderful it is that I get to go to a job I love every day, how wonderful my family is, and how blessed I am to be alive and to have my life. These thoughts evoke feelings of daily gratitude in me and I feel grateful and happy every day. Reprogramming my brain has taken time. Yes, I am still living in Bakersfield, California and I still work with the same employer that I was working with eleven years ago; but I'm happy now. I'm at peace with myself and with life. So, you ask, what has changed? *I* have changed because I have learned to own my past and present and, most importantly, I identified my *why*, found my purpose, and have reprogrammed my brain!

Reprogramming my brain has been a conscious effort. I have chosen to make small helpful changes in my thinking, over time. Choosing small encouraging thoughts to repeat over and over has resulted in a crucial shift in my thinking. I've chosen to dwell on the positive things when life gets tough and my lows start to drown me. I must be upbeat. *You* must be upbeat.

I recently experienced several stressful events in my life. During the Cedar fire in Kern County, our family cabin was in danger of burning down. Our insurance company informed us they planned to cancel our policy in six weeks and new fire insurance quotes were through the roof. Then our electric bill was $1,000 more than expected because the inverter on our solar panels had blown up at least two months prior, leaving us with high energy bills, as well as the expensive cost of repair. Meanwhile, the company that employs me was under attack and the recipient of a lot of negativity as a result of multiple lawsuits. To top it off, my son came home from school upset because other kids were picking on him. For many people, this scenario would cause high levels of stress (several ten-pound weights being thrown on their back) and in turn lead to general self-sabotage, negativity, and a depressed state. How did I deal with it? I knew I had to shrug all of this weight off my back. I couldn't carry the weight of all of this around with me. The old me would have made this entire situation about me and my stress. The old me would have turned to stress eating and complaining to everyone about everything that was happening in my life. I would have started more fights with my spouse because of all the stress I was under. Yuck! What an unappealing way to live!

What would you have done if it were you? Would you have felt the need to complain to everyone about your problems? Would you have found yourself standing at the fridge looking for something to devour? Would you have become short-tempered with your spouse or other loved ones? These actions would only cause more stress, but all too often this is how we choose to react.

Here's how my newly programmed-self handled each incident:

#1. Cabin Danger

Thought: I cannot control a forest fire. The increased cost of fire insurance for the cabin is the cost of owning a second home. It was our choice to buy the cabin and I signed on to take responsibility for it. Also, the wonderful memories we'll have while staying at the cabin are priceless. *Lesson*: When you choose to take on more than you need, what you take on will end up taking more from you, whether physically, emotionally, or financially. Understand this agreement.

#2. High Energy Bill

Thought: It's a good thing we found out about the problem when we did. We are fortunate to have solar; because of it, we've enjoyed lower electric bills for the last five years. This is a good reminder of how beneficial solar energy is for our home. We are also lucky this did not start a fire and our home is still standing. *Lesson*: I should check out our solar unit panel once a week to be sure it's is working properly. Things go wrong and break. That is life; but they seem to go wrong and break in a bigger way when you take your eye off them for long periods of time, so it catches you off guard.

#3. Company Attack

Thought: The Company may be under attack; that means I am also under attack. Why? Because I work for this company. Sometimes, when bad things happen for an employer at a company or someone's workplace, some of the working employees will often attack the company right alongside the outside attacker. People tend to separate themselves from their employer or company of employment as though they're not impacted by what happens to their employer. *News flash:* You are your company. Every employee collectively makes up your company. If you don't feel like you're a part of your company, it's most likely because of your inner bully or because it's time for you to move on and seek new, meaningful employment you can be passionate about, either working for yourself or going to work for someone else. *Lesson*: When my employer is under attack, it is crucial for me to step up even more and be even more positive, be on point, and be even more optimistic than I currently am. I've been asked, "Why do you care? It's not like they are suing you." But the way I see it, they are suing me as well. The fact that I cash my paycheck every week is evidence that I'm just as much a part of the organization as the name on the door or the CEO. Know who you are, so that you know what you are a part of. Be proud of your work.

#4.
External Bully

Thought: Kids will pick on kids. I ended up role-playing with my son, showing him examples of some things he could do if these kids try to pick on him again. *Lesson:* My son said he didn't say anything back to them because he didn't want to be mean. Wow, what do you say to that? How wonderful! We decided that the next time a kid bullies him, he's going to smile and say, "I'm sorry you feel that way," and then he's going to somehow compliment them, and say, for example, "I like your shirt."

> *"A positive attitude gives you power over your circumstances
> instead of allowing your circumstances to have power over you."*
> –JOYCE MEYER

You must change the way you think about things. If you think with a stressful mind you will feel stress. You must allow yourself to find an understanding, a solution, for what is happening in your life in order to eliminate the potential of a negative sting that it carries with it. You must learn from it, stay positive, and grow!

"The human mind is our fundamental resource," a quote from John F. Kennedy. Our mind houses the lessons; we just need to search our mind for them, be open to them, remember them, and apply them. It is vital that you say positive things to yourself every day. You need to allow your brain to absorb the good in the midst of all the negative noise.

Use your imagination for a minute. Think of your brain like a dry sponge. Now picture a dry sponge and two bowls, both filled. One bowl is filled with clear, healthy water and the other bowl is filled with thick, fatty, black oil. The water is living water, clean, clear, and healthy. The oil is unhealthy, a poison. If you put the dry sponge into the living water and let it sit there long enough, what happens? The sponge absorbs all the clean, clear, healthy water, right? Now if you were to take the supple sponge and place it in the yucky, thick, fatty, black oil, what happens? There is not a lot of poisoned oil that can be absorbed, right? Like that sponge, when you fill your brain with the good stuff, the healthy, pure, positive, nourishing, good stuff, the black yucky poisons of the world will have a hard time sticking to you. Your mind has no room for it because you are filled with the living joys of your life.

Now, what would happen to that sponge, supple with all the healthy, clear water, if you left it sitting out and don't touch it for just a day or two? Would the sponge still be as supple? Would it still be as full of the healthy, clear water? No, it would not. And if you immersed your sponge in the bowl holding the black oil what would happen? Quite a bit of that poison would now stick to your sponge, you left room for the negative to enter. That's analogous to why you have to keep filling yourself up with the good stuff *every day!* When you stop working on each aspect of your life, you're leaving the good stuff unattended and sitting out. That's an invitation for the bad stuff to come in and attach itself to your life. You must keep doing the good to keep the good in your life. Keep filling up with good!

Since I've reprogrammed my brain to maintain a tremendously positive outlook on life, I continue to keep my sponge supple and full of all the good in life. As a result, my goals and dreams seem to be within reach. As I continue on this successful journey of increasingly reprogramming my brain, I confidently share with you that this will work for you as well.

The process starts with making small mindful improvements over time. These alterations will not seem big and by themselves may not even look significant; but if made consistently over time they accumulate and provide a powerful positive force, which will change the way you think and consequently act. We must choose to look at the glass as half full, not half empty. We must stop thinking that the grass is greener on the other side and instead, start caring for and watering our own grass. Don't take your blessings for granted. Look for the good in your life and you will find it. You must choose to think this way consistently, day-in and day-out, continually reminding yourself that things are good and that you are moving in the right direction. Powerful messages become robust over time. If at any moment, you feel that your life is not progressing, all you have to do is slow down, stop, and decide to make one small mindful adjustment at a time, keep repeating it, and then make another adjustment and repeat that one too, and so on. Make a choice to change your thought patterns in life and practice those thoughts over and over.

How do you do this? First, **identify** what is bringing you down. Are you putting off exercise? Are you thinking of how much you dislike the gym? Are you thinking about how hard it will be to wake up early and go? What thought patterns do you need to change, so your daily patterns change? What thoughts are constantly bringing you down? Do you continually tell yourself that you can't accomplish something you crave to achieve? Do you know? You must change your thoughts to change your actions.

Maybe you drink too much and the alcohol you consume has started to consume you? After all, if you think about it, excessive alcohol consumption does not add value to your health. It does not add much value to your career and in does not add value to your pocketbook. It may even hinder your relationships. So, it should be a priority to limit excessive drinking. You may be thinking, *it's easier said than done, Anna!* You may think it's impossible to limit or even stop, especially if you're drinking way too much and alcohol steers your life. Do you associate a glass or a bottle of wine with kicking your feet up at home? Does the thought of a martini or a pitcher of beer creep into your head when you think of getting together with friends? Do great places to drink crowd your thoughts when you think of a night out? Do you see a pattern here? To be clear, drinking alcohol, in and of itself, isn't necessarily bad or good; you just need to be mindful of how it works for or against you.

So, how do you start to make the small changes that will eventually eliminate alcohol from your life? First, stop buying alcohol to have at home. When you think of kicking your feet up, replace that bottle of wine with something else. Second, if you spend time around "friends" who are always drinking, stop hanging out with those friends, or choose a different hangout location, or a new activity that will discourage drinking. Third, remind yourself that drinking does not enhance your life and find something to replace alcohol with. Start a new hobby, or like I did, I replaced alcohol with sparkling water and kombucha drinks. I loved beer and the sensation that comes with drinking all the tiny bubbles. So, when I decided I wanted to enhance my diet, I started by replacing my one beer a night with sparkling water or a kombucha. Beer was not consuming my life, nor was it hurting my career or relationships but it definitely was not helping any area of my life. And the fourth thing you must do is reprogram your thoughts about alcohol! Identify the moments when you think about drinking, replace them with other positive thoughts, and remind yourself of how alcohol is a negative in your life and is not helping you reach your goals.

What is interfering with your life? When you have something that is consuming your mind, taking all your mental attention and paralyzing aspects of your life, whether it be alcohol, food, sex, work, a person, or anything else, you need to minimize its presence and hence, the problem. You can do this one adjustment at a time. Again, I ask, what is consuming you?

Another tool to help you overcome the consuming element in your life is using **visualization**. Visualize your life without the detrimental effects it is in. Visualize how good you'll feel when you make these changes. What does it look like? You must pair your new mindset with visualization and positive messages. The moment you choose to change, to go down a new path with guided direction, you can tell yourself, *"Things are looking up and moving in the right direction. Change is up to me and I am strong!"* You have to give yourself positive self-talk with visualization. Visualize, give positive self-talk, take action—the combo is invigorating. You must truly believe in the change. You must reinforce positive statements over and over again. You must hold yourself accountable by reminding yourself of your, *why,* and let your *purpose* drive you to your ultimate goal.

You must *take action* and fill yourself with good information if you want good results. Keep your sponge supple. Encourage a new thought process by picking up positive books that help you focus on what you want; read them, build new skills, and work towards the future you dream of. Fill your mind with positive tools and learn new strategies to be successful in all areas. Remember you can't just work on one aspect of our life; you must be mindful and touch on all aspects of it.

When you are mindfully working on all areas of your life by putting so much good in, you are bound to get good out. This may feel overwhelming because I'm trying to get you to open up your mind. I want you to see that if you are after true self-improvement, you need to juggle all aspects of your life simultaneously and use positive self-talk to make your hard work stick. *Be your own cheerleader!*

The final piece to this reprogramming and visualization-action combo is to then reflect on how good you feel after you make a change whether it's eating a healthier breakfast, thinking about how good you feel, or taking a morning powerwalk. Absorb the positive and let it wash over you. Remind yourself every day of the wonderful feeling your positive actions are bringing you; that will encourage you to stick to constructive actions. Reflect on what you have accomplished; the little things are important.

List a big you have:

Now clear your mind, take a couple calming breaths and visualize how you will get to your goal. What does it look like when you reach your goal. Where are you when you reach with goal? Who are you with? How do you feel inside? Now think, what positive daily self-talk is needed for you to stay on track and continue moving forward with that goal? How do you hold yourself accountable? What does accountability look like to you?

What action steps/daily patterns will you take or change in the following areas of your life to reach this big goal:

Physical life:

Nutritional life:

Financial life:

Spiritual life:

Family life:

Work life:

Take time to visualize and reflect in all areas!

"The mind is everything. What you think you become!"
–BUDDHA

Love

You know how people say you have to love yourself first before you can love others and truly be happy? I have a different take on this. You can't just say, *"Love yourself."* I believe to truly be happy and love yourself you have to fill yourself with loveable thoughts, skills, and actions. It's hard to love something that is identical to what you don't love. It is hard to love an empty or negative person, even when that person is you.

My psychiatrist did have one thing right when he told me I needed to learn to love myself. The thing he had wrong was the approach. He gave me, pills, and said, *"With these pills you can now love yourself."* Telling me I would be happier and love myself by swallowing a pill is like telling someone to learn to love an ice cream sundae with dirt on it. You can't just love the dirty ice cream by saying, *"Love the dirty ice cream."* You have to get the dirt off of it first. You can't just learn to love yourself by saying, *"Love yourself."* You have to take action.

Before you can love something that you don't like, that something needs to change. In my case, that something was me. I needed to change before I could love myself. Do you love your *whole* self? What areas of your life have dirt you need to wipe off?

To get yourself to the point of truly loving yourself, you first have to visualize the change you want, then implement new daily positive actions that will move you toward that change, and do them over time. You must treat your body with respect and fill your body with nutritious food and your mind with nurturing, thoughts. Once you get that ball rolling you will be on your way to truly loving yourself. Remember, have patience as you fill yourself up with loveable actions and thoughts that readjust your life and begin to reshape it.

In the past, when I was always focused on the thought that I was depressed, I directed my attention to the self-help section of Barnes and Noble. I remember that while looking for books in the self-help section, I would feel small and closed off. It was as if I had to play the victim while looking for a self-help book. I was missing the opportunity to truly develop myself in all areas that would help me gain valuable insight and valuable skills on what I loved to do. I was too focused on my depression, on my handicap, and I kept filling myself up with self-pity, and what do you think was coming out of me? *Self-pity, of course!* Who enjoys someone that's full of the "poor me" attitude? *Not me!* So how could I expect myself to love me when I was filled with self-pity? I couldn't. I was in a catch-22: the more I focused on the negative (my depression), the less happy I became. I wanted to love myself, but there was only self-pity to love. Since I couldn't love my negative, victim-self I finally had to take ownership of my self-pity and take control of my thoughts and actions to move towards a better me. I started doing this by improving my personal and professional self by building skills, creating positive daily thoughts and patterns, and building relationships with the right people.

Let me tell you how I began reshaping my life with love for myself. First, I started reading. I shifted my mind so I would understand and appreciate the power of books until I came to love reading. Mind you, I started to read even though in the past I decided I didn't like reading. I had to change my neuro-association with reading. I had to take the negative association I had with reading and turn it into a positive association. This time around, I realized that reading was powerful and I told myself that I would become more powerful by taking time every day to read. So, I began reading books on leadership and business, which was ideal for me as I lead in my current job and I loved learning the art of making deals. I also love helping people and leading people towards becoming their very best, and the more I helped others become their very best, the better I became and—wonderfully—this hasn't ended. Additionally, I enjoy being involved in different business opportunities and learning from others, so enhancing my knowledge in these areas was important to me. I was never able to grow in these areas before by just reading the self-help books. As I slowly started to grow through reading, it became easier to love reading and I loved this type of growth, because books are full of knowledge and you have control of what you put in your mind. Read more and you will become stronger!

To make yourself more loveable you must stop self-pity. If you allow yourself to continually play the victim, you are the only one to blame for feeling like a victim. You have the power within you to change your life and blossom into whatever your heart desires. You are whatever you satisfy yourself with. Just as if you satisfy yourself with candy and unhealthy food, you will always be unhealthy, so too, if you consume yourself with self-pity, you will always feel self-pity. If you focus on the fact that you are the true bully in your life and that you can kick that bully's butt at any time to find happiness and success, you will kick that bully's butt and take control of your life. As the saying goes, "where focus goes, energy flows." You want your energy to flow to things that will move you forward towards a more *happy-whole-you.*

Before the next exercise, I want to share with you something I learned from my pastor. I found myself standing on the steps of his church because, once again, I was off track and needed guidance. I again searched outward for guidance, but this time I was much wiser and chose to look to God. I didn't revert to the negative outlets I had used in the past. I didn't look to partying or alcohol, nor excessive shopping, or pill popping, or even the self-help section at the bookstore. I looked to God and asked him to work through me because I had resumed bullying myself. I'd stayed away from a physical church for over a year at that point and had been ignoring my spiritual side for some time. As we know, ignoring any aspect of our *whole* life, like our spiritual side, will result in overall deterioration and fuel our inner bully.

During that church visit, I asked God for forgiveness, which meant I was also asking myself for forgiveness. The funny thing here is that I believe you cannot ask God—or anyone else—for forgiveness regarding anything until you have forgiven yourself and are ready to move on!

I remember sitting in the back of the church on that Sunday morning, crying. If I'd seen someone cry at church in the past, I'd think they were weird; I couldn't understand it. I'd wonder if they'd killed someone or done some other horrible thing. I'd think, *everyone makes mistakes, there's no need to cry in public at church!* Yet here I was, crying in church. I came to the realization that my life was not up to me alone; I was simply screwing everything up. I wanted to be influenced by something greater than myself. I had to be better for better things to happen. That day, in his sermon, the pastor said, *"God doesn't call for bad things to happen to us, but sometimes I think He steps aside to allow bad things to happen in order to help change us."* There it was! As long as I continued to bully myself, God would allow bad things to happen to me, but He would allow it so I could learn from it. I needed to learn from my past lessons. I needed to reflect on them and learn from them. I'll bet writing this book is part of my lesson.

As I sat in the back-pew sobbing, I remember the pastor said something like, *"If you know you have been off-track and you want to be forgiven, look up at me and we will know that is your true heart's desire."* So, I looked up and the weirdest thing happened! I actually felt all the ten-pound weights, the heaviness that I had been carrying evaporate! All those weighted mistakes just lifted off my back and I felt weightless for the first time since I could remember. I truly felt the weight coming off and leaving my body and the emptiness, sadness, and regret that had polluted my soul washed away. It was an incredible experience, a bizarre but wonderful feeling. I walked out of church that day with a newly found inner peace added to my toolbox of lessons.

Remember the sponge we talked about? The day I walked out of that church, I resolved to keep my sponge, soaking wet with clear, healthy water every day. I had the best intentions. Yet, again, after a couple of years, I began to neglect that sponge and leave it to dry. I found myself once again on autopilot. I stopped filling myself up with good things and just started going through the motions of life. Does that happen to you? It's not that I was doing bad things; I got comfortable and simply began to neglect the positive choices I'd been making. I started to drink a few beers during the week in place of the sparkling water. I made poor food choices. I began working extra hours at my job, which cut into my workout time. On the weekends, I chose to sleep in rather than go to church. As you can guess, the 10-pound weights started to add up quickly, once again, and my supple sponge was steadily drying up. I was back to focusing on the negative. I had to implement focused action steps to help bring me forward. I could feel myself slipping backwards. I didn't want that so I had to change my thinking, set new goals, and focus on the good stuff. I did just that!

> *"You're going to go through tough times—that's life. But I say,*
> *'Nothing happens to you, it happens for you.' See the positive in the*
> *negative events."*
> –JOEL OSTEEN

It is easy to find that you've gone off track and that your thoughts and actions are less than loving. Take a moment and identify what things you constantly find yourself neglecting or even focusing on, hourly or daily, in a negative way that doesn't encourage self-love. What you put in your mind matters. What do you saturate your sponge with? If you're having a burger, does your mind say, *"This is going to make me fat?"* or *"I need fries with this too?"* When you should really be saying, *"This burger is going to nourish my whole body and it is okay that I eat this; it will satisfy my hunger."* Having a negative thought when eating something can create guilt, followed by shame. If you make a decision to eat a less-than healthy burger, own it, be okay with it, just resolve not to do it often. Remember, leading a *wholistic* life is not about perfection.

We can get distracted by many things that we focus on obsessively, and often those things perpetuate self-hate. Maybe you focus on food, constantly distracted by thoughts of what you'll eat next, or how much you'll eat that day, or perhaps how food will make you feel. Maybe immediately after you eat, you feel guilty or you want to exercise, but don't. If you allow those thoughts to consume you, you have allowed food to damage your self-love. If food were to occupy your mind for the majority of the day, you would be allowing food to continue to control your life; all your energy would go to food, robbing you of the chance to enjoy other daily activities and work towards 100% self-love.

I used this example of food because I had a client who came to me seeking advice on how to overcome a food addiction. He disliked himself because of how he had allowed food to dictate his entire life. He couldn't truly love himself while repeating this behavior he hated.

Be careful what you are focusing on. Your focus can turn into an addiction. *Focus wisely!* Maybe it's not food that consumes your mind; what does? It could be thoughts about sex, money, social media, exercise, a person... virtually anything. Too much of anything is unhealthy and can devour us.

Can you identify something that consumes your focus and tries to distract you loving yourself completely? Take a minute to think about it. What is it? Is there more than one thing?

Let me share with you some simple strategies you can use to break the cycle of poisons that erode self-love. All it takes is for you to remind yourself to change your focus. Say to yourself, *"I am changing my focus, directing it onto lovable thoughts and actions that I am proud of."* Ring out the black oil that wants to stick to you!

Here are some of the best action steps I've taken to change my focus when I get stuck on one thing. I know that they're effective. I still draw from this list to help get back on a positive note with myself. Sometimes you may need to do more than one of these. There are times, when I am way out of alignment that I have to do all ten things on the list. Try some of them and make a mental note of how you feel after you've changed your focus:

- Replace your focus with a new thought or action;
- Listen to an upbeat positive song;
- Call a friend;

- Go for a quick walk;
- Change your scenery, if you are inside go outside;
- Take 5 deep breaths and smile as you breathe out;
- Read a good article or blog;
- Organize something around you;
- Send a positive message to a co-worker or someone from your past;
- Do a few push-ups (or try to);
- Stand by a tree or flower and appreciate nature;
- Take a couple deep relaxing breaths by focusing only on your breathing;
- Help someone else or do something nice for someone else;
- Call your coach.

Did any of these work? Did you feel better? Which activity on the list works best for you? Keep practicing these strategies over and over again until your mind remains glued to the positive self-loving thoughts and actions that draw you a positive self-image. This process takes repetition over time, but it does work!

> *"Find a place inside where there is joy,*
> *and the joy will burn out the pain."*
> –JOSEPH CAMPBELL

Mixed Signals

A few months ago, I heard about the concept of *neuro-associations* in an audiobook by Anthony Robbins and the concept struck me. Neuro-association describes the phenomenon of having feelings associated with things and people that are in your life. Your brain associates feelings with both and is a perfect example of why you need to change your focus at certain times and keep your mind saturated with the positive. Let me tie the concept back to what you are working on: namely, reprogramming your brain and changing your focus from the negative to the positive.

If you are not careful, the communication lines in your brain during neuro-association can get crossed causing you to program your brain improperly. For example, if you are always focusing on food and feel guilty about that, your neuro-association will cause you to feel guilt when you think about food; food equals guilt. The example that Mr. Robbins gave spoke to neuro-associations as it affects relationships. After a long stressful day, you get home. As soon as you walk through the door you see your spouse. You're carrying stress from your day and feeling this stress when you see your spouse. Your spouse may be smiling and happy to see you, but all these negative stressful feelings from your day are weighing you down inside. When this happens day after day, what do you suppose you start to feel when you see your spouse? Yup! You start associating your spouse with stress and negativity. This doesn't happen after the first day or the tenth day. However, continually feeling stressed after work, then going home to see your spouse while you're still filled with those feelings of negativity can, over time, negatively impact your relationship.

When your stress levels are high and you're transitioning or "winding down," be mindful of what you do and who you are around, especially if you have a stressful job. You don't want to start feeling negative feelings towards your spouse or anyone else because you have a stressful job, but it does happen. You must be proactive and recognize the possibility for a false neuro-association by making adjustments. When I have a stressful day, I've learned to let my spouse know I need ten to twenty minutes of "alone time" when I get home or I sometimes say, "Can we just not talk for a few minutes?" This allows me to go distract my mind so I can change my feeling from those of negative stress to something calmer and more relaxed before I join him. Lately, I find that I don't have to do this as often as I used to because I've become aware of how my feelings towards something else can impact my feelings toward someone or something completely unrelated and I simply no longer allow external feelings to control my overall mindset for an extended period of time.

Your brain is very powerful. As a human being, your emotions and feelings control what you do, what you say, and how you feel about yourself and others. You need to start associating yourself with positive things, positive actions. When you begin to do this, you start to love yourself more. Remember, nobody likes—let alone, loves—a person who pities themselves and is always saying or thinking, *"Poor-me!"* We associate bad feelings with people like that and want to stay away from them. People are attracted to happy-healthy people. If you are to love yourself and be attracted to yourself, you need to start associating yourself with positive actions and activities. To do this you need to take action and do more positive things in your daily routine. When you begin to change your daily habits so that you engage in more positive actions, you will start to associate yourself with positivity and success and love will follow. Remember it isn't hard to love a happy-positive person. What is stopping you from becoming that person?

"People often say that motivation doesn't last. Well, neither does bathing—that's why we recommend it daily."
–ZIG ZIGLAR

Take Action for Growth

It is amazing that you, more often than not, are the reason that you don't reach your goals and full potential. Jim Rohn has suggested, "We are the only creature on this planet that doesn't grow close to its full potential." I agree. We have the power of choice and the power of our choices influences our feelings and our feelings can make or break us.

Just think what it would be like if other livings things had your power of choice. What if a Sequoia tree decided it was too tired, too sad, so it decided it wouldn't grow its roots any deeper or its branches any wider? The Sequoia would not be thought of as a magnificent tree, it would just be an average tree or even less than average. What if the animals in the forest decided they were too sad and too tired and didn't feel like hunting for food? Of course, they wouldn't survive. What would happen to the food chain? What if all the flowers in the world decided they didn't want to bloom? All those beautiful colors would be missing in our flowerbeds and other living things would not be able to dive into the flowers' pollen in order to live to their full potential.

You see we are different from other living things because we have the power to choose. This power is a double-edged sword because we have too many choices, so often we make choices that screw things up for ourselves. We get in our own way and we don't reach our full potential. I have this poster of an orange basketball on an empty basketball court with a quote by Wayne Gretzky that reads, "You always miss 100% of the shots you never take," Why do you stop taking shots? Why do you quit before you begin? You will never reach your full potential if you choose to not take action.

For a long time, I wanted to do something powerful to help others. I wanted to take a shot but I was too scared to pick up a ball because I might have missed the basket. I wanted to write a book and create cool lectures that would inspire people to be better. I wanted to inspire people to better their health, their finances, their relationships, and most importantly, to better themselves, get rid of their inner bully, find self-love and be their true, happier-self. I even wanted to do this for myself before I truly knew how! It was a "want," a "wish." It was a thought that I had; but a thought I never took action on.

Why had I been thinking of doing great things like helping others through writing, lectures, and trainings, yet had never acted on them? Because, even as strong as I had become, that inner bully that lies dormant inside of us all was—and is—still in me. It's nowhere near as strong or as powerful as it once was, but it's there. I found myself listening to the what-ifs the inner bully poked me with until I couldn't tolerate being poked any more.

Do you have dreams and ideas; projects you want to accomplish, but haven't even started taking action on them? Why? You get in your own way! You bully yourself! You bully yourself with excuses and negative thoughts, and you choose to listen to your inner bully. Rather, you need to motivate yourself to work harder and keep trying. Jackson H. Brown, Jr. said it best, *"Opportunity dances with those already on the dance floor."* Don't let your inner bully take you off the dance floor of opportunity.

My inner bully used to stop me from getting on the dance floor with comments like, *"No one is going to read what you have to write. You'll probably spend all this time working on something that no one cares about."*

But guess what? The more I wrote, taking action towards this book, getting out there and dancing, the less the bully has appeared.

As for my speaking engagements? I'd think things like, *"No one is going to show up to hear me speak! You haven't done anything too special, or extremely great or unique quite yet."* Wrong! I took action against this negative thought. I started volunteering presentations and developed my skill. Soon I was booking speaking engagements and I haven't looked back since. The worst thought I would tell myself was, *"What if you try and you succeed in getting your story out there but no one cares and you end up failing?"* My response to the bully? *"What if one-person cares? What if two people care?"* We all have lived a different life; therefore, we all have different lessons and stories to share. It is important that we remember we all have something to offer.

Have you ever put yourself down before you've even begun? Do you ever have thoughts like I had? The *what-ifs*? The what-ifs kill dreams. The what-ifs kill high goal setting before you even begin. Erase all your what-ifs, except the one what-if that you should always remind yourself of: **What if I don't try?** What if you don't try, if you don't take that shot, if you don't get on the dance floor? Then what? You are just standing still and if you stand still too long, you just might get run over.

> *"If you hear a voice within you say 'you cannot paint,' then by all means paint and that voice will be silenced."*
> –VINCENT VAN GOGH

I had created a lot of negative thoughts that I let suppress me and allowed to keep me at a standstill. These thoughts killed my dreams before I even had the chance to try to make any of them come true. I had to change my way of thinking. I had to reprogram my brain and set a new focus. I had to pick up the ball, take a shot, rebound, and keep shooting.

My new way of thinking sounds something like this, *"Who cares if I fail? The only true failure is not trying at all."* I also started telling myself, *"I believe as long as I learn from this process and grow into an even better me I will have had success,"* and, *"Keep shooting Anna! You will hit the target!"*

You are better off trying a hundred times and failing ninety-nine times than trying only once and failing or not trying at all. Like Albert Einstein said, "I have tried 99 times and have failed, but on the 100th time came success." You have to change the way you think to allow yourself to move forward. Don't give in. Don't give up. Keep trying!

> *"There is no failure except in no longer trying."*
> –CHRIS BRADFORD

After I finally began to do all the things I've shared with you here, I started to achieve every goal I'd visualized. I began transforming my life. I continually remind myself of my *why* and allow my *purpose* to drive me. I *visualize* what I want and I take *action* against my fears. I continue to *reprogram my brain* to have positive, limitless ideas and thoughts. I put *small daily action steps* behind my vision and fill my mind with *positive thoughts*. It has been a most beneficial process and a process that I will continue every day.

As I continued to work on myself, I reminded myself that my dreams remain no more than thoughts until I combine action with my dreams. Nothing will happen and nothing will change unless you begin to change your actions. Once you combine purpose with action, you begin to create your destiny. My purpose to help people has driven me to write this book and it is part of my destiny to share it with you.

> *"A wise man gets more use from his enemies*
> *than a fool from his friends,"*
> –BALTASAR GRACIAN.

Get Outside Your Comfort Zone

As a human, you tend to gravitate towards your "comfort zone," that zone of your life in which you don't have to change yourself or work very hard, the zone that allows you to feel satisfied, relaxed, and able to run on autopilot. Though you're standing still, your comfort zone gives you the illusion that you're on track or even having a needed rest. But you know that's a slippery slope. When you get too comfortable and fail to try new things, set new goals for yourself, and continue to grow, you start falling backwards in every aspect of your life.

You must not get too comfortable in any area of your *whole* self if you want to grow in all areas.

When you think of participating in an activity, even when exercising, you usually choose something you're good at, something you have past experience with. You don't usually pick something that you know nothing about or something that is so hard that it would make you uncomfortable and take a great deal of time to learn. We all like easy; we like comfort.

People tend to do the same thing when it comes to food. We go for comfort. Historically, we're usually inclined to choose foods that are higher in fat and sugar, because these macronutrients create chemical reactions in the brain that make us feel good and satisfied, for a short period of time. Or, we choose dishes that remind us of happy times. During my childhood, my mom made "chicken-stuff" at Christmastime most every year. That food therefore created a sense of comfort and satisfaction due to my neuro-associations. Now, whenever it's time for the holidays, what do you think I prepare as a main dish? Chicken-stuff! I am not a great chef, so this feels comfortable to make. Do you find yourself eating the same foods, even if they are not very healthy, because they bring you comfort? What are those foods?

We also like to stay in our comfort zone in making and keeping friends. We tend to enjoy being around people like us. *Comfort—Comfort—Comfort!* We like people that think like we do and like to do the same things. This has its pros and cons. What do you think the pros are from hanging with like people? What do you think the cons are?

During my master's degree program, I had a class in which we discussed various leadership styles, qualities, and traits. Our professor said that one of the biggest mistakes people in higher leadership make is to hire a team of people who are just like they are. He said it is a common phenomenon that hurts organizations. This seems very logical to strive for a variety of different minds with different strengths, but my professor was right on the money. We do gravitate towards people that are like us in our personal and professional lives. To compensate for this tendency, we need to be more mindful of who we bring to the table in our lives.

> *"We live in a wisdom-based economy and your ability to bring the right people into the right conversations—to see beyond one's job title and job description—is an absolute must."*
> –GLENN LLOPIS

The one area in which you don't have to worry about choosing like-minded people is your family. Families are so diverse and so interesting, considering they all share similar DNA and have many traits in common. Families have unique individuals within them and family members can be all over the place. The best thing about family is that you can't pick them; you get what you get and you seem to work it out. I know that I got the characteristic of being a hard worker from my family, but does that mean everyone in my family is a hard worker, are some even workaholics? Can I learn from the hard worker, the not so hard worker, and the workaholic? *You bet!* It is good to have them all. I know my caring, compassionate heart is so strong because of my family, but does that mean that everyone in my family is caring and compassionate? Could some of them be insensitive and off-putting? *Absolutely!* But I am fortunate to experience people on both sides of the spectrum. I believe that a lot of my strengths are due to the diversity of my family members. Your family members may be nothing like you, but you learn from them all because of those very differences between you. You can use those lessons you learn to be more open to society in general. Diversity is good for growth.

I love meeting new, interesting people who are different from me. We may not share the same interests but I can learn something from them. I challenge you to step outside your comfort zone and build new uncomfortable relationships and always be ready to learn from different people.

Stepping outside your comfort zone also means you need to banish the *"what-ifs."* We have discussed the negativity of the "what-ifs" in earlier pages. Life used to seem a lot less complex when I carried around all those negative *"what-ifs"* in my head, as long as I thought *"what-if,"* I wasn't challenged to make change in my life, so I remained comfortable. I may have been unhappy but being unhappy became my normal and therefore had become "comfortable." Every time I would think about changing, I felt a sense of exhaustion because changing takes energy. So, I remained the same, stagnant, until I became restless in that comfort level and was compelled to do something.

We all need change to grow. I knew I had to change the thoughts in my head to move forward and I did change my thoughts by reprogramming my brain and my daily patterns. Then I took it a step further and began to write down those positive thoughts and changes I was making, I could see it on paper and in my mind. This visualization was extremely powerful. Do you write your thoughts down? Once I put my thoughts and goals on paper I felt vulnerable, I reminded myself failure was not possible because I was growing. I kept telling myself, *"You have to try. Things take time. Be consistent. Just try!"* Write down the changes you desire in your life. You can use this same thought to produce those changes.

The truth is that failure can't happen when you challenge yourself with positive intentions, thoughts, and goals. I never wrote my thoughts down before because I kept telling myself I would fail and, of course, writing them down takes time, energy, and creates a sense of realness. When you are in your comfort zone you don't have much extra energy because you have no drive to draw energy from. When you write down your goals, take *action* to implement change, and keep pushing forward, you will find you are energized.

If you're holding yourself back from doing something, it is because you have thoughts or fears of failure. *Stop bullying yourself!* Your only failure is that you allow your internal bully to keep you in your comfort zone and have control over you and your life.

Can you imagine if Taylor Swift, Steve Jobs, or even Henry Ford stopped pursuing their dreams because of the *"what-ifs?"* What-if they refused to get outside their comfort zone? Each of these individuals had their own *"what-ifs,"* their own fears, and their own external bullies and the madness of their own internal bully (recall that the internal bully takes the words of the external bullies and makes them their own). I bet they all became uncomfortable at many points in their careers. Thank goodness none of them accepted defeat nor allowed themselves to quit before they started. They all chose to continue to pursue their dreams. I can't imagine going for a power walk without my wonderful Taylor Swift playing. Her anthems give me a pep-in-my-step and make me feel youthful. Imagine if there was *no Apple*! I know you can't. Do I even need to remind you that Henry Ford gave you the chance to get a sweet ride? You see; the only thing standing in the way of your greatness is you. You can do much more when you give yourself the encouragement to lean in, get uncomfortable, and go for it. You don't grow or learn from not trying. Don't let the fear of the "what-if" stop you!

> *"Your time is limited, so don't waste it living someone else's life.*
> *Don't be trapped by dogma—which is living with*
> *the results of other people's thinking.*
> *Don't let the noise of other's opinions*
> *drown out your own inner voice.*
> *And most important, have the courage*
> *to follow your heart and intuitions."*
> –STEVE JOBS

Move Your Body, Move Yourself Out of the Way

Remember that earlier I shared with you I ran cross-country and track for my university? I definitely got in my own way back then. I allowed poor choices directed by my internal bully to get in the way of proving that I was more valuable than a walk-on athlete. I regret my failure to keep a positive mindset for it hindered my physical ability. As a result, I was not a very strong runner during my college years. However, many years later, when I was finally able to get out of my own way by practicing the strategies I have been sharing with you, my running improved dramatically.

I've had more running successes over the last five years than I ever had in college, despite the fact that I have way more going on in my life. I have run faster at every age between the ages of twenty-eight and thirty-four than I did between the ages of eighteen and twenty-two.

As a mom with far more responsibility, I have remained in far better physical shape and mental shape. Why? Because I changed my mind set; I got out of my self-destructive, poor-me comfort zone.

At the age of eighteen, I worked so hard to run a 5k (3.1 miles) in nineteen minutes; at the age of twenty-eight, I ran that same 5k (3.1 miles) a hair over seventeen minutes and I have ran many other 5k's under seventeen and a half minutes since. What an improvement! I've also been able to run many 10k's, half marathons (13.1 miles), and marathons (26.2 miles) at a pace of roughly five and a half minutes to just over six minutes per mile. This is crazy considering that back in college, I was a lot younger, hadn't gone through pregnancy and childbirth, and I only had obligations to myself. Yet, back then I still allowed myself to get in my own way of success when I had the freedom and youth to do anything. If you are presently in your youth, don't waste it, if you are older, you always can improve and become better than you were.

I share this because I want to show you that when I was able to finally get out of my own way, I could achieve the successes I had only wished for earlier in life. Did you notice I said, *"Wished"* for? Remember, you can wish away all you want, but action is needed for growth and action is needed to turn a wimpy wish into a strong reality. There is a big difference between saying, *"I wish I were a faster runner,"* and saying, *"I am going to get faster by training hard and consistently getting up every morning at 5:00 a.m. to put in the work."* Do you see the difference? I desperately wanted to prove myself back in college, and I worked hard at exercising but exercising was the only aspect of my life that I worked on. I failed to work on the other aspects of my life during that time—among them, my nutrition, my mindset and my relationships. I was not juggling all aspects of my life and therefore I felt weighed down and off track. I was only focused on the physical exercise. I neglected to live a *whole* life. As a result, my actions were moving me away from actualizing my *"wishes."* I am thankful I *stopped* this negative behavior at the age of twenty-eight when I redirected my inner bully. This was a great lesson for me.

If you have a wish, stop working on only one aspect of your life. To make it come true, take action and participate in all aspects of your *whole* life!

I want to share more of the reasons why running didn't work for me when I was in college and why it works for me now. Things that may initially seem positive can end up getting in your way if you let your inner bully use those things against you. When I was running in college, I used to tell myself I *had* to run, and I *had* to run so many miles, and I *had* to, *had* to, *had* to until running was no longer enjoyable, it was a chore I'd given myself. If you are an aspiring runner, please *do not* think of running as a chore, or something that you *must* do. Anything you feel you have to do, *"or else,"* can quickly come to have negative neuro-associations. Things that you want, or need to do for your growth should be viewed in a positive light. They must be perceived as, *"I get to do this!"* or *"I want to do this!"* and *"This is making me so much more whole."* Stop saying, *"Ugh, I have to do this,"* getting that negative-yucky, *"have-to feeling."* Change the negative thoughts and feelings, into positive ones. Maintain a positive neuro-association with anything that you know will move you towards your goals.

Today, I view running as my daily dose of happiness, my daily dose of "Prozac," my daily dose of therapy, and my daily dose of gaining clarity and creativity. I no longer view running as a chore or something I have to do. I look at it as my positive therapy, my sanity, and a way to heal my spirit. There is this amazing clarity about life that I get when I'm running. When I run I don't even listen to music; my positive, motivational thoughts are my music!

I also run with a running group, which holds me accountable if the inner bully ever tries to slow me down or stop me from continuing my regimen. Yes, as much as I love the runner's high, I still can sometimes be vulnerable to getting pulled back down by my inner bully. Sometimes, my inner bully shows up in the morning when it's time to get out of bed, but it lasts only for about 2 minutes, because I jump right out of bed with a smile, as though I've just defeated a great monster. Do you ever experience something similar? You know, when the world is waiting for you to start accomplishing your goals and you just don't want to get out of bed because the bully in you is saying,

"Stay in bed. This is way more comfortable!" When that happens, quickly get out of bed and smile!

"To enjoy the glow of good health, you must exercise."
–GENE TUNNEY

I must share with you just how important movement is. A little bit of daily activity goes a long way. A little boost of high-energy activity, every day, will keep your body youthful and rejuvenate it. I'm sure you've noticed (especially if you have kids!) that kids run from point A to point B for almost everything. I can call my three-year-old daughter into the kitchen and she'll come in sprinting from the other room. How much fun and how funny would it be if for one evening you made an agreement with your spouse, kids, partner, roommate or whoever you live with that you will run from point A to point B all evening. I bet you'll start laughing the first time you see your partner dashing towards you. Wouldn't it be great if it were more socially acceptable for adults to move more, to run, jump, hop, and skip along throughout the day, like kids do? What if at work you and your coworkers decided every time someone is coming back to their desk from, say a bathroom break, they had to run? Seriously, how many people would joyfully laugh alongside you? There is greatness in the playfulness of running and moving more. Think of some fun games you can create at home and work to move more and put them into action.

I know that running has truly saved my life in many ways. The lessons I have learned through the sport of running (as well as other sports) have been priceless. You may not be a runner, but you can become a runner or a power walker. Do you think you could be either of these? Your answer should be, *"Yes, of course I can, why not?"* If that wasn't quite what you were thinking, then go back and don't allow yourself to think of any reason why you can't. Instead, start giving yourself all the reasons why you can. Be open to trying new experiences and new things to better your life. Start with a 1 minute walk and a thirty second jog and repeat this over and over, then build from there. You will be amazed at what giving yourself a nice run or power walk for twenty, thirty or forty minutes will do for your mind and body, not to mention that your inner bully hates a good workout! *Cardiovascular fitness is in and a bully life is out!*

> *"The reason I exercise is for the quality of life I enjoy."*
> –KENNETH H. COOPER

It is Up to You!

Choices

The choices you have made are a direct reflection on how your life is unfolding. You make thousands of choices very quickly: the choice to hit the alarm clock for the third time, the choice to wake up and go for a jog or to watch the news, the choice to eat a donut or a grapefruit or both, the choice to wear pants or shorts, the choice to make yourself a victim of life with an it's-not-my-fault attitude … the list goes on and on. The choices we make configure who we are, what we do, and who we become. You are who you are today because of every single choice you have made up to this very moment. Let me say that again, **you** are who **you** are today because of *every single choice* **you** have made up until this very moment. You must take responsibility for *all* **your** choices. Choose wisely!

Some of you do not take ownership of your choices. You may blame your life circumstances, where you grew up, your family, your lack of education, the job you have, or a thousand other things. Some of you blame others for how you are feeling or why you did or didn't do something. You cannot blame anyone or anything for your life. Ultimately you are who you are, because of *your* choices. Whether you choose to react or respond to someone, or something; how you choose to treat your family, your friends, or a stranger; how you choose to spend your money; your food choices; what you choose to wear; if you choose to exercise, how often, and where. All these choices add up and make *you*, **you**!

Don't look for ways of dodging responsibility for your life. You can cop-out and say you are who you are today because of, say, your upbringing as an example. This cop-out would ultimately credit everything around you today, as being there because of your childhood, suggesting that you had no control over your life back then and that your life is not your own today. This is not only foolish, it's wrong! *Your life is yours!* Sure, outside factors might influence your choices, but ultimately, *you* make the choice and *you* choose the action to take. I could try and blame those who bullied me at school or my second-grade teacher, but how would this help me? I had a choice then of how to respond to the events that happened in my life and I have a choice now. So do you!

Life is fluid and is constantly moving and changing, and you are constantly making choices as to how you will respond to your life's changing events. Thinking and acting as if you have no control of how your life is unfolding is equivalent to wallowing in self-pity. When you are immersed in self-pity, you do not own your choices. When you don't own your choices, you provide space for your inner bully to appear, take control, and make choices for you. Remember, you either choose to bully yourself or you choose to lift yourself up. There is no middle ground.

Austrian, Victor Frankel once said, "Between stimulus and response there is a space." The space he spoke of is our power of choice. Choose wisely because every choice you make will have multiple outcomes. *You are in control!*

"There are three constants in life… change, choice, and principles."
–STEVEN COVEY

Money Choices

Let's discuss choices in terms of money. Most people avoid having "money talks," but then, hey, I'm not like most people! I find it interesting that while it is considered impolite to discuss finances, it's perfectly okay to talk at length about one's diet or exercise routine. Is there a difference? Financial health is a critical piece in your puzzle of *wholeness*. Discussing the impact of the choices you make about your money lends itself well to a discussion about "choices" because money is a tangible; you can see it, track it, count it and feel it. What you chose to do with your money says a lot about you as a *whole* person because your money choices impact every area of your life; your health, your mental well-being, your relationships, and, of course, your financial health.

Some of you allow money to define or label who you are. Some of you may even argue that the amount of money you have determines your happiness. I learned the value of a dollar at a young age. My mom actually had a spreadsheet and would keep track of every dollar she would loan out to my siblings and me. The five dollars she lent me for the movies, and the seven dollars she furnished for a school item, both would go on the spreadsheet. This served as a great lesson for me at a young age teaching me to live within my means, and to always pay back what I borrowed.

Fast-forward to adulthood and the same principles apply. I have credit cards that I use—but at the end of every month I pay back what I borrowed *in full*. This very simple concept seems lost on many of us for whom credit card debt, and debts in general, are the norm.

The choice of how to spend your money and how to use credit cards is completely up to you. How are you spending your money? How are you using your credit? There are many things you choose to buy that may add little value to your life and the lives around you. I don't believe that enough parents consider how profoundly their money choices impact their kids. Many don't give a thought to how you're spending impacts your *whole* environment. You need to be mindful of how you choose to treat money. Be aware of how important you make money in your life.

Unfortunately, I used to spend my money on useless things. I didn't spend all my money on junk, but enough so that I was left thinking I didn't have enough money to do certain things. You see, sometimes when you think you're choosing one thing, you lose sight of the fact that you're actually making many more choices. For example, when I was choosing to spend my money on things I didn't need, I was also choosing not to save that money for things I did need and for adventures I wanted to take down the road. Our choices have a compound impact. Remember to take some time and track your spending. You will uncover some habits and spending patterns that you may want to change.

> *"Wealth is the ability to fully experience life."*
> –HENRY DAVID THOREAU

Non-Real Choices

Choose to get rid of the junk you have and stop buying more junk. Choose to save your money. You know that how you spend your money directly impacts the quality of your life. There are other choices in your life that impact the choices you make about your money and vice versa. You need to rid yourself of some of these other poor choices that drag you down: trash magazines, "reality" or negative TV shows, people who don't lift you up (and I'll bet these people are costing you money as well! Think about what you do and what you spend your money on when you're with certain people), books with no value (some of you may argue with this and I respect your need to read novels, but please ask yourself if they're helping you move towards your goals, and if they are, then keep on reading!), negative music, and any other negative thing that causes you to reach into your wallet without yielding a valuable, positive return on the investment.

Time is money and I used to spend a lot of time and money on the junk I listed above. I first started paying attention to celebrities in my freshman year of college and began reading trash magazines. I religiously bought *US Weekly, People, In Touch Weekly, OK Magazine,* and any other magazine sitting by the checkout stand with a freshly airbrushed model on the cover and a negative tag line. I would be in the checkout line, grab one of these magazines, and dive into the content and pictures as if they were truly newsworthy. *OMG!* These magazines were filled with nonsense! I remember looking at a *"Who wore it better?"* section of a magazine, with photos of two celebrities wearing the same outfit with percentages by their picture. The big question was, *"Which celebrity wore the outfit better?"* I ask you, *who cares, right?* But for some crazy reason, I did! *But why?* I surrounded myself with all the trash magazines and the trash TV shows, like *TMZ, The Insider*, and *E news*. The magazines and TV shows all told the same irrelevant stuff, so I was getting the same poor message from multiple outlets. Talk about repetitive toxic messages going into my brain! *Yuck!* The information I got from these toxic sources made no positive difference in my life. Their negative impact? They all stole my time, my money, and polluted my brain. Yet, it was my choice to expose myself to this. ***You become what you satisfy yourself with.***

I began to think my life was so boring in comparison to these perfect celebrities, *a false image I was seeing!* During this time in college, I developed a skewed view of a healthy body image. I began to think my body was deformed and ugly because I didn't look like Jennifer Lopez or every Victoria's Secret model. To top it off, I was surrounded by students who were skinny cross-country runners while I had big thighs and a big booty. I think the only thing that gave me a little self-confidence was that Jennifer Lopez had a big butt, and had made big butts popular. I was stuck between yearning to be skinny and wanting to keep my booty. This is completely silly! I wasted unnecessary energy on my obsession with impossible, superficial perfection. I was consumed by the toxicity I surrounded myself with.

I know that what I thought was real, was an aberration. I was looking at a composite photo of spray tans, professional makeup and expert airbrushing. All the other benefits of being a celebrity—like having your own nutritionist, exercise guru, chef, nanny, housekeeper, wardrobe designer and hair and makeup artist—cause you, the average person, to think you fall short. One of my Canadian friends said to me once, *"You Americans are so obsessed with celebrities, it's weird."* It *is* weird! Why should you pay more attention to, and be more concerned with, the lives of celebrities or anyone else's life than with your own? You move backwards when you do that. *But then why do you do it?* Because you are giving your focus to something outside your own life to distract yourself in order not to deal with the changes you need to make. It is a lot easier to neglect yourself and stay in a false zone of comfort by using celebrity news or any other outside distraction to remain stagnant and maintain the attitude of self-pity.

We now have the phenomenon of *the Kardashians, The "Real" Housewives* of whatever city, *The Bachelor*, and many more "reality" trash TV shows to keep the madness alive. *OMG! Stop the madness!*

I didn't finally let go of my celebrity drug intake until about four years ago. I was at the doctor's office and I had just found out I was going to have a baby girl. What a special moment! As I sat up after the ultrasound, I noticed a magazine devoted to health on the table with a young lady, airbrushed to perfection on the cover. Something in me snapped and I felt a rush of anxiety. I did not want my baby girl to see that cover! I did not want my daughter to believe that looking like that is either a real goal or what will bring her happiness. I couldn't wait to get home and throw out every trash magazine I had. I immediately stopped watching all the celebrity news shows, stopped watching "reality" shows, and cancelled our Direct TV service. I shared with my husband my belief that I was addicted to TV and had developed a false sense of reality. He definitely wasn't happy about losing our Direct TV service but he understood the problem and my concern and I got him Netflix and Amazon Prime to make up for it. As a bonus, we began saving money every month by canceling our satellite service. I also stopped buying trash magazines. Now, when I glimpse any celebrity news, I laugh. I am so proud of myself; I feel like I've defeated another monster! I purposefully developed a negative neuro-association with trashy magazines and trashy celebrity news shows, and it feels great!

A quick little side note: While waiting in the checkout line the other day at Target, I looked at all the chips, candy, and trash magazines that are available in the checkout line. They all have something in common: all of them are bad for your body, mind, spirit, and pocketbook, not to mention how bad it is for our kids to see this junk as they wait with us in line. These checkout lines are filled with trash: women in bikinis with their bodies airbrushed and with seemingly flawless skin (what a lie); headlines that read, "Cheating," or "Divorce," or "Weight Gain," or "Broke," or "Train Wreck," and many other negative words that instill a toxic film over your mind. Wouldn't it be great if at every checkout line there were healthy snacks and positive images for us to emulate? I hope that the many conversations I will have with my kids explaining that these are false images and only junk, sticks with them so they are able to go through the checkout lines ignoring all the trash they'll see around them. They are too good for that junk. *You* are too good for that junk. *Don't buy it!*

> *"It is our choices… that show what we truly are,*
> *far more than our abilities."*
> –J.K. ROWLING

People Choices

Now that you understand why you should save your money and stay clear of trash magazines and trashy TV shows, you need to know why it's important to choose to surround yourself with upbeat people. I found I used to surround myself with people that were always making excuses. Guess what? I was one of those people! I, too, was always making excuses. These people were negative and I was negative, so we gravitated towards each other. I also found myself associating with people who, though neither negative nor bad, didn't push me; people on autopilot who weren't growing, which in turn meant that I, like them, was stuck on autopilot and not growing.

I truly believe that most people are good and want to be better, but the reality is that not all people are willing to take action to do anything about it. I decided I don't need to be around "most people." I need to be around happy, successful people, people who push themselves to become better and who want to see me become better along with them. This is not the same as having a friend who believes in you and wants to see you do well and keep pushing to be better while they sit back and are stagnate. Not a passive cheerleader in the stands. *No!* Seek out people who are also challenging themselves to grow and become better. A true friendship should be a pact: you take care of yourself and push yourself to be better, and I will take care of myself and push myself to do better, so that we are not dependent on one another and we are both striving to be better while providing the other with the positive support needed. This makes for a great win-win, healthy friendship!

You must be mindful of who you give your time to. Have you heard the theory that you are an average makeup of the five people you spend the most time with? Who are your five people? Do they inspire you? Do they challenge and push you to do better? Do you aspire to be like them? Write down the five people you spend the most time with and their major strengths and weaknesses. Then write down all your strengths and weaknesses. Do you see any similarities?

Name	Strength	Weakness
1.		
2.		
3.		
4.		
5.		
YOU		

> *"Remember, the choices we make today*
> *shape the people we become tomorrow."*
> –VICTORIA OSTEEN

Self-Improvement Choices

This brings us to our next "get out of your own way" practice: *Study and read!* Yes, this is coming from the same person who was shamed for being a poor reader. I hated reading throughout school. *Why?* Because I was lead to believe I was a poor reader. Whatever the excuse may be, the truth is that you don't have to be super smart or a speed-reader to read. You just need to choose to read good stuff. You can also choose to study by listening to CDs, by attending seminars to improve yourself, or by enrolling in an on-line class. The bottom line is that you must continually fill your mind with good stuff! Keep growing and challenging yourself. My car is a rolling university. Every day I choose to listen to personal development CDs while I drive. I'm also constantly rotating a couple books that I'm reading. *Why?* Because to become better, to become more, you must always be learning.

The beauty in reading books, is that someone else has taken mountains of their own time to put together lessons they have learned and you get to scoop up all that knowledge by lying on your couch and taking it in without having to experience the pitfalls you otherwise would. Search and find what you want to learn about. The information is out there and it is up to you to capture it. What do you want to capture? Do you want to have a better diet? Then choose to study nutrition and take some healthy cooking classes. Do you want to be a better parent? Choose to study parenting and take some parenting classes. Do you want to grow your own business? What do you think you should choose? Interview successful people, get the books they read, study and take some classes. You must keep growing and setting new goals for yourselves. Through reading books, listening to CDs, and attending seminars and trainings, you can grow and become more. Choose to be a student of learning and you will always be growing.

> *"An investment in knowledge pays the best interest."*
> –BENJAMIN FRANKLIN

I just finished a class at Berkeley called "The Science of Happiness." You may ask why I would be taking a class on happiness. It was a simple choice: I like being happy! I want to keep my feelings of happiness. Remember we are what we surround ourselves with. If you surround yourself with learning about happiness there is a good chance you will feel greater happiness. Jim Rohn says, "When you are searching for something and you find it, capture it!" He is so right. Capture your findings. Don't just read it and leave it. Take it with you. Practice what you have learned and infuse the lessons with your purpose.

I will sometimes listen to an audio book over and over again. Why isn't once enough? Because I need to capture what I'm learning! My steps to learning are as follows: I search for it, I capture it, I practice it, I retain it and sometimes I teach it, and repeat the cycle. Be a student, be a reader, and become a teacher who still reads and shares what you know. The cycle should never end, no matter how successful you become!

> *"Make the most of yourself, for that is all there is for you."*
> —RALPH WALDO EMERSON

Choice of Fear

Don't allow your emotions to control you. You need to be disciplined to differentiate between listening to your true heart versus listening to your mind. Your mind is where your inner bully awaits. Your inner bully likes to conjure up fear. Remember, what you allow your inner bully to tell your mind can become an emotional expression. If you believe your inner bully when it tells you that you'll fail, you will have a fear of failure before you have even started. Don't think about failure unless you want to feel failure. Think success! If you think you will succeed, if you tell yourself you are succeeding, you'll feel excited and motivated to move forward. You have to trust your true self. Your time is now. Don't trap yourself. Don't push your dreams back. Don't let your inner bully paralyze you with fear.

Overcoming fear can only happen by loving yourself, loving what you do, and doing what you love. You must allow yourself to do what you love every day. Don't hold back! Your time is limited and it takes a positive mind to do what you love day-in and day-out. We all spend most of our lives working.

Why not do what you are passionate about and become what you truly want to be? A good start is to change your thinking about your current job. You may say, *"I can't do what I love to do every day because I need to put food on the table."* I challenge you to change your mindset.

To begin with, you must change the way you view your job. Think of your job as something you get to do when so many others who don't have a job and would love to take your place. Not too bad after all! You need to go from, *"Poor me, I have to,"* to *"Lucky me, I get to!"*

Fear held me back from reaching my dream of being a writer. Fear held me back from being a great runner. Fear held me back from being happy. Fear will kill your dreams and fear will paralyze you and prevent you from ever beginning. Fear told me I'm not smart enough, I'm just average and I will probably fail. That fear was my thoughts. That fear was in my brain. That fear was my inner bully. Don't let your inner bully take over your direction.

> *"Growth is never mere chance; it is the result of forces working together."*
> –JAMES CASH PENNEY

Here's another quick story: I recently went to hear Dan Thurmon speak. I was scouting Dan to see if his message would be a good fit for a particular group of educators. Wow, what a great fit he was! He was phenomenal! His talk was more than a presentation—it was an outside-the-box, extraordinary performance. The audience was as entranced with his every word as he actually juggled, rode a unicycle, and did flips on stage during his talk! Most importantly, he was speaking about living life "Off Balance on Purpose," which is the name of his New York Times bestselling book. As I watched Dan grab the audience's attention and listened to his message, I got very excited. The principles and ideas he was sharing were similar to those I've been writing about in this book. I was excited to meet with him after the show and share with him that I understood his message well and that I was pursuing the goal of doing the same thing he was doing: namely, speaking to large groups and delivering an inspirational message with tremendous grace and confidence. He was living my dream!

I am not a juggler (although I can juggle) nor do I ride a unicycle (although I can use a pogo stick and jump rope at the same time) but I yearned to engage an audience as he was doing. I wanted to learn from him. After his performance, I sat down with Dan to discuss the possibility of him speaking to our staff on a professional development day. He was very friendly and open to the idea. Most importantly, he has a high regard for educators. So, he was all in and I was delighted. We would work out the details later.

That decided, I shared my passion for self-improvement with Dan. I told him that I was writing this book and that a lot of his message was similar to what I was trying to deliver in my book: motivation, encouragement, growth, and helping change people's mindset. He congratulated me on the process of writing a book and then he handed me a signed copy of his book, *"Off Balance on Purpose."* I was so anxious to read it that I dove right into it. At first, I thought, *Wow! This is great stuff!* But by the time I got to chapter six, fear began to set in and I started to feel a sense of failure. His book was written so well! He'd explained a lot of concepts way better than I had. My inner bully came out. *"Anna, just stop writing now. Your book is nothing compared to this. Your book is horrible!"* That's right! For a week, afterward I was fighting the bully in my head. I had to work to change the messages I was choosing to receive in my head. I kept writing! By doing what it is that you fear, you are taking action against that fear and thus, your fear will be reduced.

Regardless of what becomes of this book and even if no one reads this book, I'm writing this book for me. This book is for my kids. This book is for my friends. It is my hope and dream that this book will reach complete strangers and help them defeat their inner bully, but if that's not to happen, I know that at the end of this process I can be proud of having completed this. *I am proud of doing this. This is not an easy thing and I have already learned a great deal from this process!*

So, you see, fear reshapes your thinking and tries to stop you from moving forward if you don't get serious and get control of your fear. You must stand up to your fear. For me, this meant I had to read my own words, capture them and practice them so I could share them. I had to push that fear aside so I could stand up for my goals and myself. I kept reading Dan's book and writing more. I took action against my fear. You must take positive action against your fear.

Replace fear with your *why* and your *purpose*. Provide yourself with thoughts of *I can, I will, my time is now!* You must continue to repeat these phrases over and over again in your mind. Repeat these like the repetitive flashing neon signs in Times Square or like the running ticker tape of stocks at the bottom of a newscast. These messages must become a permanent imprint within you.

You can push fear out of your mind by reading books like this one. By saying daily affirmations to yourself, by finding and doing what you love, and by facing fear head on. Do whatever moves you closer to your dreams every day. Giving into fear is giving up. Don't give up!

Here are some action steps to help you stomp out the fear that is holding you back. Remember these action steps must be done every day. These steps do not take a lot of time, but like one of my mentors, Jeff Olson, says, "It's easy to do and it's easy *not* to do."

- Read a few pages of a motivational book every day;
- Say three positive things to yourself upon rising in the morning;
- Say three things you are thankful for before you go to bed;
- Face fear head on with action: keep doing what you are fearful of;
- Share your goals and dreams with others.

"Fear is only as deep as the mind allows."
–JAPANESE PROVERB

Choice of Stress

One choice we have every day is the choice of feeling stressed or not. This concept can be hard to swallow for a highly-stressed person. Many people that choose to be highly-stressed have created a compound effect of stress by making many small, poor choices. Let me share with you a few bad choices stressful people choose—choices I use to choose:

1. They do not get enough sleep;

2. They choose to do work they do not love;

3. They eat unhealthy;

4. They over spend;

5. They over caffeinate;

6. They don't take time for meaningful relationships or take meaningful relationships for granted;

7. They are pessimistic;

8. They do not practice deep breathing;

9. They hold grudges.

These are a few things that I have done as an over stressed person and things I notice that other stressful people choose too. The thing about all of these is they have a compound negative impact on your life. We truly never choose just one thing. Choosing one thing is really choosing multiple things, if you think about it. For example: If every time you hear a coworker talking about a new weight loss plan you choose to laugh, chuckle, and make comments like, "I like being bigger," or, "I like to eat my fast food," or, "Getting up at 5:00 a.m. to workout is insane." Do you choose to make smart comments to someone trying to improve their life? When you chose to do this you were choosing to put that person's goals and dreams down and you are choosing to allow yourself to think that being unhealthy is okay. You can't lie to yourself.

The compound effect of our choices impacts our stress levels profoundly. If you choose to skimp on sleep, you are then choosing to be tired the next day. If you are choosing to eat unhealthy then you are choosing to increase your chances of getting ill, missing more work, and making less money. Your stress starts with your choices.

If you want to create good stress you must make better choices. Maybe you choose to start walking for 60 minutes every day. Did you know taking 60 minutes to walk every day is only using up 4% of your total day? Did you know choosing to do this also will decrease your risk of heart disease, diabetes, and weight gain. This is a positive stress choice.

To overcome negative stress, you must replace your negative behaviors with a positive behavior. Instead of skipping your afternoon sales calls, replace that with committing to make two calls every afternoon. Instead of following negative posts on social media, follow positive posts and post your own positive information. Instead of picking up coffee on the way to work, make your own at home to save time and money.

Identify two or three choices you make, perhaps on a daily basis, that create negative stress. Now commit to replacing these negative stressors with something more positive. Continue these new positive actions over the next month and see how you feel. Keep in mind that not all your stress is negative. Stress can provide you with energy, too. Examples of positive stressors are exercise, deadlines, competition and learning something new.

It is vital to acknowledge and understand that what you choose impacts your growth. Decide what stressors you need to add or eliminate in your life. There are so many choices that we make every day, though we do not give much mindful attention to them. We need to choose to be mindful of what we allow ourselves to consume, be it food, people around us, information, thoughts of fear, and anything else in our environment. If you choose to fill yourself with positive self-talk and greatness, you will have greatness. Eliminate negative stressors. Remember, stress is self-induced.

"The greatest weapon against stress is the ability to choose one thought over another."
—WILLIAM JAMES

Grow

Goals

Congratulations, you are reading this because you believe in personal growth. You know it is important to have *goals* because you grow when you are setting goals and reaching towards them. To reach your goals, you need to visualize reaching the goals you set for yourself. You need to set goals so high that they may seem unreachable, goals that others may laugh at and discourage you from believing you can achieve. You need to set goals that will pull you up higher than you could have otherwise imagined. You are better off aiming extremely high and falling short, then aiming lower and falling short. *Aim high!*

I challenge you to think back in your life to somebody who may have set goals higher for you than what you thought you could accomplish, maybe a teacher or a coach. A part of you may have believed there was no way you could achieve the higher goal they had set for you, but in fact you did. Can you think of a time when this happened? Does it make you smile?

Don't be scared to set high goals for yourself right now. Isn't it great to have people challenge you and push your goal-setting higher? All too often, it seems these people were only around in our youth. As an adult, you still have to reach for the stars. Set higher goals for yourself and surround yourself with those who have higher expectations of you than you may have for yourself. Don't be an average goal-setter. Average people set average goals and *you* are not average. Successful people set above average, extreme goals. *Be an extreme goal setter and your life will be anything but average!*

> *"Our duty, as men and women, is to proceed as if limits to or ability did not exist. We are collaborators in creation."*
> –PIERRE TEILHARD DE CHARDIN

One thing I have learned is that every goal requires the same ingredients to reach towards it. Every goal demands a plan from you, determination, hard work, and continuous effort. I have always made it a firm policy never to tell someone to make his or her goals more "practical." I believe that too many people do this all too often with their children. A child may say they want to be a professional athlete, but their parents may say things like, "You need to be more realistic!" We try to make them change their (laudable) goal. Why? Why would we do that, when what they need to do to reach their goal is so good for them, namely, hard work, determination, consistency, and so on. I embrace all the goals my kids have as I embrace my own goals. Don't put a ceiling on your goal-setting. Don't put a ceiling on your kids' goals either. It is one to the easiest ways to limit yourself and your children. *Be limitless!*

Imagine that you were looking for a dentist because you needed a tooth pulled and you had two options. You could choose Dentist A, labeled "average" or Dentist B, labeled "above average." Which would you pick? Silly question, right? No one wants average. In truth, is there really such thing as "average?" You are either moving forwards or backwards in life, right? But when I think of something average I think it is right in the middle, not too good and not too bad. Do you want a dentist labeled "not too good and not too bad?" No, right? Don't you want the dentist that is recognized as "excellent," "best of the best," "number one?" To earn any of these "labels," you cannot set goals that are average. To earn a higher mark, you must set high goals.

If you have a hard time setting high goals because the internal bully gets in the way and tells you, *"That is never going to happen,"* or, *"Get real, be practical,"* you need to use visualization techniques. Setting high goals and visualizing you achieving those goals helps kill that inner bully. Visualization is a powerful tool; you must choose to use it or lose your vision! Many professional athletes use visualization as part of their training. Not only do they train their bodies through strength and muscle memory, they train their minds to see victories before they even occur. That's right! You, too, need to train your mind to see positive things before they happen. I use visualization every day of my life and it is a high yield exercise I do with my clients. The strongest vision you set in your mind is what you will gravitate towards in life. Take in the positive and see yourself achieving your higher goals every day.

"To come to be you must have a vision of being, a dream, a purpose, a principal. You will become what your vision is."
–PETER NIVIO ZARLENGA

I've shared with you the lack of confidence around reading and formal education I've had to battle because I allowed my second-grade teacher to steal that confidence from me. However, my tenth-grade English teacher spent extra time with me and told me I was smart. She had high expectations for me, which made me set higher goals. When she read my work, she'd often tell me how great a writer I was. She knew I struggled; but she encouraged me with confidence in my ability. She'd return my papers and tell me to work on them, to improve them, because she knew I could make them better. She'd never return a paper to me and say it wasn't good enough; she'd say, *"I know you're a better writer than this and I know you can do better."* Allow the encouragement of your past mentors to be a reminder to keep you pushing higher.

Before tenth grade, I never dreamed I would go to college because I never thought I was smart enough. Mrs. Grundstrom instilled in me the confidence that I could go to college and be successful. I just had to keep trying and set my goals higher. Today, I have a master's degree and I have served as a teacher for over a decade. I have continued my formal training and have earned many additional certifications. Having had a nurturing role model and a caring leader, like my tenth-grade teacher, has allowed someone like me to draw from past expectations and set higher goals for myself. Had I taken the easier route, set my goals lower and hoped to simply just graduate from high school and get a job somewhere, settle in and allow life to take me where it may, it would have been a huge mistake. I would have allowed a life on autopilot to destroy my potential. If you have not had a mentor like I had, please use my example and let me be the mentor you never had. You can do whatever your heart desires. You must work at it. You must keep trying and continue to work on you. Dream big and set high goals. Anything is truly possible!

"When it is obvious that the goals cannot be reached, don't adjust the goals, adjust the action steps."
–CONFUCIUS

Earlier I shared with you my run-in with Dan Thurmon and my desire to be a speaker. For the longest time, I have wanted to get up in front of groups and share words of inspiration, hope, and guidance. I wanted to provide people like you with encouragement and lessons that would help you avoid the pains and pitfalls I have gone through in my life. I wanted to help those of you that feel hopeless and those of you who let your inner bully dictate your life. I wanted to help you find hope and solutions that improve your *whole* life. This goal started as a thought that was followed by fear, and negative self-talk. *"That's never going to really happen. Who is going to listen to you? Everyone is going to judge you, and what if you forget your words? You should just be happy where you are and keep doing what you're doing! Only super talented, smart people can be speakers and you are not one!"* This is what the typical cycle of what negative self-talk sounds like. It is fueled by fear, self-doubt, and the lack of continually setting higher goals. Your inner bully loves this and this cycle causes you to feel as if you are at a dead-end. It will paralyze you. I paralyzed myself with this negative self-talk. This debilitating tornado of thoughts kept me from taking action towards my goal of becoming a motivational speaker.

To get out of this tornado of negativity I had to consciously draw upon my past motivators and remind myself of those who have believed in me. You can draw upon your past motivators when you need a push in the right direction too. I got to the point where I couldn't take being average anymore and I had to break out of my autopilot life. I'd gotten comfortable and started to do things that were chipping away at any growth I had developed. I was all too aware that I had stopped adding challenges in my life and I caught myself in the "meantime" autopilot space. So, I started to push towards my dreams once again. I began saying daily affirmations: *"I can do this!"* and *"I will do this!"* I started to visualize myself speaking in front of large and small groups of people. I visualized myself on stages, in classrooms, and in conference rooms. I visualized people smiling, laughing, nodding along and even taking notes as I spoke to them. I visualized people shaking my hand, thanking me afterwards. I could *see* myself in front of a hundred people. I could see a hundred-people clapping and cheering in joy because the words and experiences I was sharing touched them. I visualized reaching this high goal, drew on motivation from my past mentors—and now it *is* actually happening! I have reached my goal!

You must laugh away negative thoughts that try to creep into your mind. When negative thoughts try to stop you, you need to be armed with skills that will defeat them. You must strengthen your belief system and say, *"Ha-ha fear and self-doubt! You have no room here."* Remind yourself of why you want to reach that goal, follow your purpose, and grab motivation from your past lessons.

Remember, you have to *visualize* yourself reaching your goals and whatever else you want in this life. When you can imprint this picture in your mind, your mind starts to recognize it *as if it is already happening!*

"Attitude is a little thing that makes a big difference."
–WINSTON CHURCHILL

Time for another quick story: I went to my first Laughing Yoga class last week. Our instructor said, *"Even when you fake laughter, your mind and body have the same chemical reactions they would have if you were truly laughing."* I found that an interesting statement, though a little odd at first. Actually, I thought the whole class was odd at first. The flyer advertising the class read, "Enlighten Your Life with Laughter." I had envisioned it to be a classroom setting with the instructor in front of the room telling jokes and doing various things to make us laugh. I was expecting a handout of some sort and a *PowerPoint* presentation. I was ready to take written notes. Boy, was I way off!

When the class started, the instructor asked us all to come up to the stage. She then shared the fun fact that our brain and body doesn't distinguish between genuine laughter and fake laughter. I stood in a circle with five other women, who were strangers. The instructions given: *"Go up to every person, and just look them straight in the eye and laugh out loud as hard as you can with them!" What? Awkward! Was this lady for real?* She was for real and I did as we were told. Not only did we laugh in front of each other, we did so standing no more than four to six inches away from the stranger's face. *Yikes!* But guess what? It worked! I spent the next fifty minutes fake laughing with women I didn't know and, though I felt extremely uncomfortable the entire time, when I walked out of there I felt substantially lighter—and much happier. I wasn't sure if I was feeling like that because I couldn't wait to call my best friend and tell her about this awkward class or if it was because of the class itself. But does it matter? I kept smiling for a long time after that class was over and I am smiling even now as I share this with you. It was a fun class. I highly recommend that you try a laughing yoga class.

I'm sharing this story with you because it all started when I began to imprint a "fake" laugh in my brain and continued imprinting over and over again for fifty minutes. Thinking back to the image of fake laughing so close to strangers' faces still makes me laugh. It's just like when I visualized my goal of speaking before a group. I started with a goal followed by visualization, then started practicing my speaking abilities (taking action) in front of one, two, three, four or more people. Every time I spoke in front of these small groups I'd fake it, as though I was speaking in front of a crowd of hundreds of people. I envisioned myself talking successfully and practiced it over and over, and it came true. I have since spoken before hundreds of people. I haven't once forgotten my words—and people listened! Don't get me wrong, I still get nervous when speaking in front of any number of people, but I remind myself it's not about me, it's about giving them the message they need to hear!

Visualize what it is you want. If you want to laugh more, visualize yourself laughing, even fake laughing out loud. If you want to be a stronger speaker, visualize yourself giving awesome speeches and the crowd enjoying every minute of your presentation. Practice with small groups and even speaking in front of a mirror. If you want to buy a new cool car, but don't have the money yet, visualize yourself getting the money, handing over the money to the car salesman and then go test drive the car until it is yours. Whatever your wants are: set a high goal, visualize you achieving your goal, and practice your goal.

Don't stop visualizing and goal setting when you achieve and reach the goals you set for yourself. You need to continually make those goals higher and bigger. Don't settle for being "not too good," or "not too bad." Strive for being the very best and keep climbing. You may ask when is enough, enough? When will you be completely satisfied? Let me tell you that the very moment you stop visualizing greater achievements and stop pushing yourself to reach your full potential (which is limitless), your inner bully is going to reappear and influence you negatively. That's when you'll find yourself in the autopilot zone. You are not meant to be average nor are you meant to just stand still. If you stop reaching, visualizing, and making things happen in your life, you will be reminded by your inner bully, over and over again, that you are stagnant and not good enough. Don't stop your action steps. Progress keeps that inner bully at bay. When you get to the point where you can push the bully out of your mind and focus on achievement, you start to grow. Remember, life is fluid and constantly moving. Visualization, goal setting, and achieving are the antidotes to the inner bully. *Keep pushing upward!*

Here are some activities you can do to start achieving your goals sooner than you thought:

- Make a vision board;
- Write out all your goals in vivid detail;
- Visualize your day upon rising;
- Visualize and fake it until you achieve it;
- Always keep setting new goals. Never find yourself without one;
- Share your goals out loud. Let everyone know what you are working towards and even hire a coach to help you.

> *"The only thing worse than being blind is having sight but no vision."*
> –HELEN KELLER

Worksheet #4—The Dream Matrix

This fourth worksheet is your Perfect 10 worksheet. Here, you are to write out in detail what your life will look like ten years from now, using present tense. Write out everything you can possibly think of and use very vivid details. Include what you're doing, where you're living, how you're feeling, and whatever else you can think of—and want for yourself.

HAPPY.
WHOLE.
YOU.

PERFECT 10

DREAM MATRIX

www.HappyWholeYou.com

Get to Know You

If you are like most people, you may pay more attention to other people and what is happening in their life than your own. Some of you may know more about what is going on with the Kardashian family, or your best friend's diet than you know about your own family or your own diet. You may know how to get under your spouse's skin to motivate him or her to do something you want done. You may even know more about what motivates your kids then what motivates yourself. I bet you know more about how to work your iPhone than how you work. Yes, I just compared you to an iPhone. (That maybe going a little too far, but you get the point, right?) You spend more time getting to know about material things or spend more time watching someone else's life play out than your own. It is so easy to draw your focus on something or on other people, but what if you took that time to focus on yourself?

Do you know what makes you tick? Do you know how you can become great? Do you know how many times a day you have a positive thought? Do you know how many times a day you have a negative thought? How many times you say something nice to yourself? If not, why? I'll bet you can remember every negative thing that caused you frustration today and yesterday. *Why?* Why do you remember all the external negative things and allow them to shape you, yet ignore the negative things that you say to yourself and subject yourself to? You pay attention to the external environment that you cannot control, and ignore or neglect all that is within your internal environment, your mind, which you *can* control.

If you want to be great, not good, not okay, but the very best you can be, you must get to know yourself! When you get to know you, you'll be able to transform your mind, and there is nothing more powerful than a changed, positive mind. When you change your internal thoughts and behaviors to be positive and constructive, you then start harnessing the power to push towards your greatness.

> *"No bird soars too high, if he soars with his own wings."*
> —WILLIAM BLAKE

Have you ever had an argument with someone or disliked a person, then had an occasion to sit and talk with them, get to know who they truly are and what is in their heart? I'm pretty sure that once you got to know them, you could no longer have negative thoughts towards them. Have you ever found someone annoying, then discovered that they'd recently lost a loved one or that they were going through some other negative experience like cancer and your feelings about them changed, so they no longer annoy you and you felt your heart was more open to them? You experience a change of heart because you are a compassionate being. That's why I want you to truly get to know yourself and fill yourself with lovable actions. I know that once you truly do, you will love yourself. It is a lot harder to be mean to yourself and have negative thoughts towards yourself when you know who you are; when you know what, you've gone through and what you are going through. If you identify whatever it is that you are working through, learn the lessons, grow, and give credit for what you want to become, I know you will be kinder to yourself. You have to get to know yourself in order to be compassionate towards yourself. You have to give yourself credit for all you have been through and all you have grown from. And remember, as you are filling yourself up with positive, nourishing, uplifting thoughts and actions, you are making it a lot easier to know and love yourself!

What you think is extremely powerful because you become what you think. Know your strengths. Know your weaknesses, too. Know your inner desires. Know who you are, so you can become what you desire. Here are some action steps to help you get to know yourself and move yourself closer towards a happier-successful you:

- Spend time alone every day to clear your mind and reflect on your day;
- Visualize everything big and small that was great today and how you influenced that greatness;
- Visualize what you will do tomorrow to be better than you were today;
- Visualize yourself achieving your dreams;
- Get to know yourself because it's harder to be mean to someone that you know and care about.

"Our senses don't deceive us: our judgment does."
–JOHANN WOLFGANG VON GOETHE

Worksheet #5—The Future Matrix

This fifth worksheet is the Future Matrix. You have written down your "big picture" in vivid detail in the last matrix. Now take time to break down those goals into realizable parts. This worksheet presents you with a timeline where you will write out your plan for the days, weeks, months, and years to come to reach your goals. This charts your plans for right now, today, tomorrow, one week from now, one month from now, one year from now, three years from now, and five years from now. I recommend that you first write all this out on a separate sheet of paper then come back to this Future Matrix and on each line write a title that represents what you plan to accomplish in that time. Put your desires and dreams here!

www.HappyWholeYou.com

Deal with Your Missteps

Once I started to get to know myself, I realized I had a lot of issues. I allowed what others told me to mold me. I allowed fear to control me. I had to deal with the fact that I had low self-esteem. I had to deal with the fact that I was surrounding myself with negative people. I had to deal with the fact that I had an ego.

We all have issues. Once you get to know yourself, you can begin to work on your issues. One of the issues I discovered surprised me at first; I had an ego. How could someone with low self-esteem have an ego? I realized that I turned the small things I did, and the small things that happened to me into far bigger things in my head. I made them far more complex than they objectively were. *Why?* I was trying to make both myself and others think that I had more reasons to be stressed than I truly had. My ability to deal with that stress made me out to be better and more important than I was. What I ought to have done instead was try to actually be better. You see, being a misleading persona never really works because, bottom line, you can't trick yourself into thinking you are any better or bigger than you are. You may be able to trick others but you cannot fool yourself. You know if you're doing the little important things every day to better yourself. You know how hard you're really working. You know how many times you procrastinated or played on your phone when you could have been working on your goals. You know if the reason you're feeling bloated this week is that you chose to eat bad food all week. You know the reason you're not as strong at the gym this month is that you skipped a lot of workouts last month. You know if you skimped on sales calls last week and this impacted why your sales were down. You know exactly why you are where you are. You may try to trick yourself and those around you by masking your lack of good choices with expressions of stress or putting the blame elsewhere, but you know the truth.

You know that person who's always stressed because they make it seem like they have way too much to do and not enough time? It's as if they are the only person doing anything! That's their ego. I had to stop trying to satisfy my ego with overdone and overplayed excuses about my stress. It was hard. I had to stop making my "stressful life" my crutch or my fall back reason for failure, and the reason why I wasn't living up to whatever expectation of me was out there in the universe. If you see yourself as a "high stress" person, *stop now!* No one cares! More importantly, you're lying to yourself. You're only as stressed as you make yourself.

Remember the Laughing Yoga class? The lesson there applies to fake stress as well as to fake laughter. Your body and brain will undergo the same chemical reactions with fake stress as with real stress and this fake stress brings on more physical stress.

Stress is a part of life. We need some stress. The stress we feel is the result of cortisol, the natural hormone your body makes that wakes you up every morning. It is not what prevents you from being great; *you* prevent you from being great. Greatness doesn't just happen to you; you make greatness happen because of you. Accept yourself for who you truly are and don't try to embellish your stressful state; build a state of well-being!

I've heard Tony Robbins say, "People are rewarded in public for what they have spent years doing in private." Get to know yourself in private. Work on being better in private. You shouldn't have to publicly declare how hard you're working or how stressed it's made you in order to get attention; you shouldn't need that attention. Once you've done the work, you'll get that attention and good things will happen.

You have to be confident in who you are and in what you are doing. When you begin to love yourself, and do what you love, it will come out in public. It happened to me. It is happening in this book. I have had to go through all the things I'm talking about. There is nothing in all of this that calls for a very extreme, larger-than-life action. Rather, there are a lot of little things that take place over time. I've had to work on me just like I'm helping you work on you throughout this book. It may be a bit of a challenge, but it's definitely worth it!

Once you deal with your personal issues and work on yourself, you'll realize that you really do have full control over your dreams and you can reach your goals. You'll realize that only you define your limitations. You'll realize that you can become a stronger version of yourself. You'll realize that any and all the negatives you have experienced can be turned into positives as you move forward. You'll realize that you deserve to have your dreams come to fruition and that you can reach them by making small improvements and taking small action steps forward over time. You'll realize that when you know who you are, you'll become something greater because you'll know *you* and what makes you tick.

You must stop simply surviving and allow yourself to thrive. Take these action steps below and turn your surviving life into a thriving life. It won't happen overnight; it takes work, but you'll find that it's worth every step along the way.

Action Steps:

- Clear out any clutter in your external life;
- Step away from people who are negative, even if you are "friends";
- Change any negative thought into a positive thought; Example: If, in the past you said to yourself, *"I'm broke and depressed,"* (in which case, you will be broke and depressed) say instead, *"My money is growing and I am growing;"*
- Acknowledge what you are struggling with and tell yourself what you will do to improve your struggle by taking action to turn it into strength;
- Write out specifically what you want, what you will achieve, and how you will achieve it;
- Acknowledge your ego and move forward.

> *"A bad day for your ego is a great day for your soul."*
> –JILLIAN MICHAELS

Your Labels

The labels we give ourselves and others can be uplifting or destructive. You have already given yourself and those around you many labels. You may not even realize you have done this. How have you labeled yourself? Is it the label you want to represent?

The label I have given myself is complex. This is the label I want to represent: *I want to represent unlimited possibilities. I want to represent unlimited happiness. I want to be seen as someone who is inspirational. I want to be—and I am—someone who helps others become the best that they can be, and this will never end.*

Your true label is also complex. Why? Because everything in your life has significance and everything is interconnected. No one is only a jock, a mom, a musician, or a business executive. There is always more to one's label, yet we allow a simplistic label to rule over us.

Your label is always changing and evolving, just as your life is. If you stop growing in a positive direction you will start to depreciate yourself and your label begins to dwindle and shrink towards the less abundant label. Moving forward with personal growth increases your positive label and causes a positive ripple effect in your life. You are growing your positive label by working through this book.

Just as your inner bully can paralyze you, all too often, you allow society's labels, and what others think about you to paralyze you, as well. The inner bully loves when this happens because it feeds off these outside suppliers of negativity. As an example, think of someone you know who dropped out of high school. What do you think of that person? And how do you think that person views themselves?

Before I met my husband, he was living up to society's label of a high school dropout. He had begun drinking too much and was becoming involved with drugs. His reality became the labels that society tagged him with and, sure enough, his inner bully blossomed. Fast-forward years later, when, after working on his inner bully, he has been able to create a successful reality. He attributes some of this to the fact that I believed in him and didn't judge him negatively simply because he hadn't graduated from high school. I attribute his growth to him taking action and moving beyond his label. I present you with this personal example to show the importance of being mindful not to have outside labels and influences feed your inner bully lest the voice of the inner bully becomes your daily anthem of failure. And be mindful not to be an external bully, negatively labeling someone else. You do not want to fuel someone else's inner bully.

Maybe you are someone who chose to leave college to pursue something other than a degree? Maybe you wanted to get married and have a family. Maybe you wanted to go straight into the working field. Maybe you had no idea what you wanted to do but you knew college wasn't it. Society shouldn't label you a "dropout" nor should you feel guilty or "less than" for leaving school. Don't let society's label define you if you didn't finish your education and don't allow that label to fuel your inner bully. You can always go back... if you truly want to make that part of your goals and no one's education is ever finished!

Some other situations that give rise to societal labels: having a baby before you had planned to; going through a divorce; making or losing a bunch of money; battling a life-threatening disease. I'm sure you can come up with many others.

When you choose a different path, for whatever reason or a different path chooses you, you have to tell yourself: "I'm growing from this. I was not in the optimal place to become my best." You must have a more positive mindset because when you make any life change or have a life-changing event happen, your inner bully is ready to take advantage of your transitional period. Change has a way of allowing the fear of the unknown to control us and your inner bully will tell yourself, *"I've made a mistake! Or why me? Or I am a failure. I'm a loser. I will always struggle because I didn't finish school or didn't take that job opportunity or didn't do this or that."* Learn from what you didn't do and use the lesson to grow in what you are doing. Identify any negativity that may creep into your label and eliminate it. Realize that you have gone through many labels to get to where you are today, to the point where you can say, *"Yeah, I went through that, and I learned so much!"* or, *"Sure, I did that, and I learned a lot from it!"* And do not allow a simplistic label to define you. You are way more complex.

Use society's labels to motivate you, to light a fire under you, to get you to read a book like this. But don't allow these labels to stimulate your inner bully and drag you down. Accept what has been and see the positive in it all.

Own where you've been and where you're going. No matter what it was, and no matter how many labels you have been through, the key to having a happy and successful reality is to own your journey. Do not be the victim of your label. Allow the lessons you learn here to fuel your life. Most importantly, the only true label you should consume is the label you give yourself!

My label today: *"I am a happy, loving, successful wife and mother who has been through a lot of life experiences and come out of them smarter, better and able to help others because of them."* Notice, your true label will always extend beyond one word. It will be forever changing. To present yourself with a single-word, simple label is you bullying yourself. Write your true label below and be proud of it!

What is your Label? Write it out:

Action steps:

1. Repeat the label you gave yourself above daily;

2. Rewrite your label regularly (every three to six months) and see if it changes;

3. Give some of your friends and family a new label like the one you wrote for yourself above and send it to them; It would look like this:

Dear Friend,

You are the most loving, encouraging, successful, mom I know. Your ability to bring people together is inspiring. You are inspiring. Your commitment to our friendship is so loving and I appreciate you!

Love,

Me

"Spread love everywhere you go. Let no one ever come to you without leaving happier."
    −MOTHER TERESA

Your Financial Life

Speaking of labels, one of the labels you most readily tend to give yourself is a financially worthy label. As we've said, there are those of you who base your success on the amount of money you have in the bank or the worth of the assets you hold. I won't deny that your finances play a big role in your overall emotional well-being. Your financial well-being is a part of being *whole*. The inner bully can become even louder when your bank account dwindles. But you must change your mindset when it comes to money. What I mean by that is that you need to change the way you view money, use money, and react to money. I spoke a little bit about this earlier when we discussed your power to make good choices. Now, I want to share how everything, including your finances, is linked together impacting your *whole* life.

How you value your money influences how you value yourself. The quality of what you spend your money on reflects the quality of your life. How will you spend $100? If you spend it on eating out and junk food versus buying fresh healthy food it will impact the quality of your health and therefore, your life. If you spend it all on cigarettes and alcohol rather than taking your kids to a movie or the park, the quality of your life will reflect that choice as well. Choose to spend that $100 on a small TV for your kitchen rather than spending it on a new pair of walking shoes and that choice will also be reflected in the quality of your life. Likewise, choose to buy a larger house that's 65 minutes from work rather than buying a smaller house only 35 minutes from work, and there will be a difference in the quality of your life. Spending wisely and acknowledging how you spend money impacts all aspects of your life.

If you're a careful spender, does it mean you are a more cautious person in all aspects of your life? If you are a frivolous spender are you more spontaneous in life? Are you someone who almost always finds something wrong with something you've bought and returns it, even months later? Do you instantly regret what you've just bought? Do you experience mixed emotions when you've spent money? Maybe? Maybe, not? I bet there are some similarities between how you choose to spend your money and how you feel about yourself.

I can attest from first-hand experience that making more money doesn't buy more happiness. Your finances will equal happiness only when you have control over your money and that emanates from having control over your mind. As my wise grandfather says, *"It's not how much you make, it's what you do with it."* How very true!

I want to share with you the gist of an article on financial wellness that I wrote for our company newsletter.

Financial Wellness Anyone?

We all need money to survive. How much money we all make varies but it is how we choose to spend our money that determines our overall financial health.

From a young age, I quickly learned the value of a dollar. In my family, when we began 8th grade, we became responsible for buying our school clothing, our movie tickets, and anything else that was deemed "extra." My mom actually used a spreadsheet to keep track of any loans she made us and she gave us opportunities to earn money by doing chores and helping with the family business. Yes, even if I borrowed $5 to attend a school football game, that $5 went onto the spreadsheet. At the end of every week, I could see how indebted I was. I remember calling family friends to ask if I could babysit or mow their lawn over the weekend for extra cash with which to pay off my debt. I always tried to be debt free by Sunday night. To some, this may seem harsh; but the lesson it taught me about money has been priceless.

I wonder if those of you who have not grown up with such necessary lessons have learned the value of a dollar. Even if you were as fortunate as I was and had an adult give you valuable money lessons, how do you navigate through the financial world? What do you do with your money? Let's say you are a saver and end up with an extra $200 at the end of the month. What do you do with that money? Do you use it to make extra payments on your credit cards? Invest in a 401k? 403b? A Roth? You may be asking what the heck all these are and how to even begin saving $200 extra every month!

According to a 2012 Employee Benefit Research Institute survey, only 14 percent of American workers say that they are "very confident" that they will have enough money to live comfortably in retirement, and 30 percent of workers said they have less than $1,000 in savings and investments (www. ultimatecheapskate.com/). With an eye to these statistics, it is frustrating that discussions about money and finances between us is considered impolite; yet, it is perfectly acceptable to talk about our diets and exercise routines. We need to have more MONEY TALKS, people!

According to the website, CreditLoan.com, the average American—that's YOU! —pays more than $600,000 in interest over the course of a lifetime. Think about how much of that money you could avoid throwing out the window by adopting the old-school philosophy: *"If you can't afford it, don't buy it."*

What you can do NOW to SAVE BIG for the future:

Pay extra every month on your mortgage throughout the year. If you pay an extra $25 a month on your mortgage, that extra payment will mean that you'll pay off your remaining loan balance 1 year and 7 months earlier than you otherwise would, thereby saving $13,712.52 in interest over the life of the loan (timevalue.com based on a $200,000 loan, amortized over 30 years).

STOP buying coffee on the road. A 12-ounce bag of ground Starbucks coffee contains 34-six-ounce cups. So, it costs you about $0.60 to brew a cup of Starbucks brand coffee at home. (Add the cost of electricity, plus the one-time investment in a coffee maker. On the other hand, it might cost you extra gas and time to drive to a Starbucks or to idle in the drive-thru, but let's leave all the less important peripheral issues aside for simplicity's sake.) Depending on how elaborate your Starbucks order is and how large your cup, the bottom line is that you could save a bare minimum of $1.47 per cup brewing Starbucks coffee at home. If you have only one cup daily that's 365 times $1.47= $536.55 of savings per year or $44.71 every month. (Of course, more elaborate orders are more expensive which lead to higher savings.) (http://www.jsonline.com/blogs/news/249776901.html).

Invest your extra coffee money! According to the Compound Interest Calculator from the U.S. Securities and Exchange Commission, if you were to put your average minimum monthly savings of $44.71 into a mutual fund earning compound interest at a rate of 6.5% and interest is added 12 times per year, after 10 years you would have $7,614.80 instead of the pleasure of standing in line for a cup of Starbucks coffee.

Meet with a financial advisor. Get a professional opinion from someone who's not trying to sell you something. Make small changes over time. If you get a raise of, say 3%, allocate that 3% to pay down the debt that's charging you the highest interest rate. Not in debt? Great! Then put that 3% in your retirement account. The winning strategy is to make sure you're not living 3% better than you did before the raise.

Action Step: Know where your money is going. Keep track for one week every single cent you spend and evaluate where you can make small changes.

> *"Money is only a tool. It will take you wherever you wish,*
> *but it will not replace you as the driver."*
> –AYN RAND

Did you find any good advice in there? Let me share with you some ways I choose to spend my money and ways I will not spend my money. During college, I heard the saying, *"If you will live like no one else today you can live like no one else in the future."* In other words, I learned to save and be mindful of what would move me towards my goals, so in the future I wouldn't have money problems like many others. As I've gone through the last decade of my life, I've experienced what some might call "financial struggles." I simply view them as choosing to live like no one else! For example, unlike most people, for a long time, I chose not to purchase things with credit cards. Today, when I do use credit cards (I find they're a good way to keep track of where I spend my money) I pay them off *in full* every month. I've always chosen to live in apartments that were lower in cost and close to work to save on gas and time.

When I was single, I chose to have roommates to help share costs. At twenty-eight I bought my first home for $216,000. I put $50,000 down on a fifteen-year fixed rate mortgage (side note: did you know mortgage in Latin means death?). Are you wondering how I had $50,000 at twenty-eight when just five years before at twenty-three I was $16,000 in debt and making only $42,000 a year? I saved it all during my first five years of teaching. As a teacher, I was only paid for 10 months out of every year, which equaled $4,200 a month for each of the ten months. Sounds pretty good, right? Well, remember I had to take out various taxes, insurances, retirement, and I had to set money aside to pay for the months I didn't get paid. And, since my last paycheck was the last working day in May and I wouldn't receive another paycheck until the last day of August, in truth, there were three months between paychecks. I'm not complaining about this; I'm merely sharing the big picture with you. My monthly net was roughly $2,200. Still not bad, right? Well, from that, I would mail $1,000 every single month to a bank account in Michigan, for which I had neither a debit card nor checks. If I wanted to withdraw any money from that account, I would have had to physically appear at the bank in Michigan, which is why I set it up like that. It made me think twice before I spent money. So, now I was down to $1,200 a month with which I had to pay rent, electric bill, car insurance, gas, food, college loans, and all the other basics in my life. I was living paycheck-to-paycheck.

Do you know someone with the label of "living paycheck-to-paycheck?" That label can sound the same for each paycheck-to-paycheck person, but they can be very different people and can mean very different things. So, you see, financial health varies from one person to the next, even when they make the same amount of money.

Let me share with you how I did *not* spend my money. I did not get my hair done every month. I did not get my nails done every three weeks. I did not go on cool vacations and I did not buy expensive clothing. I also chose not to have any kids and chose not to have an expensive car. I did, however, make some poor financial decisions although they didn't seem big at first! My biggest financial regret is that when I started my career, I began buying more trash magazines (at about $2.99 a pop, times buying about 10 magazines a month, I wasted about $29.99 every month) and I bought trash TV (sharing with roommates, my cost about $45 a month). Right there, I could have saved $74.99 a month. This may not sound like a lot of money, but I chose to spend this amount every month for about eight years. My decision not to save that $74.99 every month for 8 years ultimately cost me a total of $7,199.04. If I had invested that $74.99 each month into a Roth IRA or 403B, and had a conservative return of 4% on that monthly $74.99 contribution for 8 years, at the end of the eight years, I'd have had $9,854.91. Wow! It really does add up, doesn't it? It all matters. I'm sure glad I stopped buying trash magazines and quit watching trash TV because I am now saving my money!

During the time I was saving $1,000 a month, I decided to get my master's degree. It was during my fourth year of teaching and I was then making about $48,000 a year, which wasn't too bad. I decided not to take out any loans. Instead, I worked out a payment plan with the university agreeing to make a monthly payment of $1,000 a month. Yup, the $1,000 I had been saving coincidentally was the same amount I had to pay to the university for eleven months. During the time I was paying $1,000 a month for my education, I sent only anywhere from $250-$350 every month to my account in Michigan. This was okay because by this time I was making a little more money and my living expenses had actually gone down a bit because I had moved and I was now renting a room from a coworker rather than renting an entire apartment. I had some extra money that allowed me to keep a buffer in my savings account.

When I completed my master's program, I got another raise upon which landed me at about $60,000 a year. During this same period of time, coworkers asked me, *"How can you afford to get a masters, when I'm still trying to pay off my undergrad loans?"* I also had classic comments from co-workers whose situations were similar to mine, as they, too, had no kids and were on the same pay scale as me and had been teaching about the same amount of time as I'd been. They'd say, *"I just don't have the time. How do you find the time to do it?"* The difference between us was that I had chosen to make time and save my money, so when the time came I was able to take advantage of the opportunity to obtain a higher education and move forward. If those other individuals had earned their master's degree the same year as I did eight years ago, today they'd be earning an annual salary of roughly $77,902. Instead, because they chose not to spend their time or money towards a master's degree that would earn them a higher wage, their annual pay today is $61,897. That's a difference of $16,005 a year! As this job comes with an annual step pay increase, the difference in pay over the last eight years between us is about $115,153. Wow! Talk about how you can turn some savings into something really big!

Another way I have "lived like no one else" is that my husband and I have completely paid off the $216,000 home I bought less than six years ago. When I purchased this home, my ultimate goal was to pay it off in five years. Over the last five years, we've had our fair share of financial ups and downs, but ultimately, we were able to pay off our 15-year mortgage in five years and two months. Of course, having two incomes has been a great boon. A bigger benefit than having a roommate to share costs is having a spouse to share a mortgage and other long-range economic goals. We also have two kids and a dog to take care of so childcare expenses, clothing, and feeding and caring for two additional little people has added expenses to our expense sheet so, it wasn't easy. But we were able to reach our goal. For the first seven years of our marriage, we were living paycheck-to-paycheck. Why? Because we had the goal of paying off our mortgage. We were able to reach it because we lived within our means and didn't spend money on frivolous things. Our mortgage had a price tag of 4.25% interest. Did you know a mortgage of $170,000 over fifteen years would cost you about $56,938.86 in interest (according to mortgagecalculator.org)? If you take that same loan and choose to spend your money on a thirty-year mortgage at the same interest rate, it will cost you $122,779.71 in interest. If you own a home you may want to look into paying it off early. With the early pay-off, my spouse and I saved over $35,000. If you add the $115,153 advantage I made by getting my masters, I really accumulated over $150,000 in 8 years simply by choosing to be more responsible with my money.

Take a moment and think of what you spend your money on every day. What are you buying that's hurting you more than helping you? If you eat fast food every day at McDonald's, Wendy's, or Burger King, you are paying premium dollars for someone else to make you food that is not nutritious. Is that fast food nourishing your cells? Is it providing you with energy or is it making you fall asleep two hours later? Is it causing you to gain weight? If you are spending money on poor quality food, do you know what it's going to cost you in the long run? Do you think about what it could cost you if you develop type 2 diabetes or have a heart attack? Simply not having the energy to do what you love doing or to play with your kids should be a wake-up call. What does this all really cost? Can you put a price tag on it?

Remember, every financial choice you make is far more complex than you think. Say you're thirsty and you choose to get a drink; you choose to quench that thirst with a bottle of soda for about $1.99 or more, plus a deposit for the bottle. You drink the soda and you feel refreshed. You're no longer thirsty. The truth is, you didn't only choose to quench your thirst, you also chose to send you blood sugar levels soaring. You chose to increase your chances for cavities. You chose to add empty calories to your diet, which will cause you to gain weight. When you gain weight, you feel more tired and when you feel tired you just want to lie around and watch TV. When you're lying around watching TV, you're disengaging from your family and friends. Maybe your kids see you sitting there, staring at the TV and they ask you to play with them and you tell them you're too tired. Your kids feel disappointed but they choose to sit down with you and watch TV, too. Now you are all sitting there, not engaging in conversation with each other, and just being blah.

We've learned that when you are making little choices, like what to drink when you get thirsty, your one choice becomes many choices. You chose a soda; but could you have chosen water? Humans tend to be creatures of habit, that one time you grabbed the soda turns into two or three or four or five times, which turns into you grabbing a soda everyday as you now associate quenching your thirst with drinking soda (neuro-association), and once you drink that soda, all the other choices that you didn't think you chose start to happen, leaving you to wonder why you have no energy, why you have gained 20 pounds, why you're now a borderline diabetic, why your health insurance premiums have gone up, why you no longer qualify for life insurance, why you feel disengaged from your family, and why you're $61.50 a month ($2.05

a day x 30 days) poorer, and your kids continuously feel disappointed that their parent doesn't have the energy to play with them, though to that child, it just feels that you simply don't want to play with them.

What we choose to do with our money has a ripple effect in our lives. Each decision is a cluster of decisions. We need to reprogram our brains to think beyond the one purchase.

Write down three things you spend your money on that you could live without:

1.

2.

3.

Now write down every possible impact that purchase could have or does have on you and those around you:

1.

2.

3.

> *"You can't be in debt and win. It doesn't work."*
> –DAVE RAMSEY

Excuses

On the road of life, you can often find yourself with an exhausting list of excuses. You may be the type of person that uses excuses in abundance yet not realize it. If you are one of these people, you probably view yourself as a "victim." You always feel like life is not fair and you have excuse after excuse for your lack of success. Excuses are what unhappy and unsuccessful people use to run away from claiming responsibility for their shortcomings.

What is your philosophy? Did you know that it is the way you think? And that life philosophy has been developed from everything you've chosen, everything you have heard, everything you have surrounded yourself with, everything you have experienced, and how you've chosen to respond to all of it up through this very moment. What philosophy have you developed? Think about it. We all have one. Is yours a good one? Does it serve you well? Can you come up with a better philosophy? Do you want a better philosophy? If you are a "victim," your philosophy has been skewed by your list of excuses. To develop a better philosophy, you need to have a healthier mindset and eliminate all excuses. You need to improve your environment. You need to have a different strategy than the one you're currently using. You need to change your thoughts, your vocabulary, your practices, and your actions. *No more excuses!*

I remember my days of unlimited excuses. During my excuse "victim" days my philosophy was to blame anyone and everything other than me. *"Life is not fair," "If only my parents paid for my college education, I'd do so much better in school"; "If only I made more money I would be happier"; "If only I didn't have to pay so much in taxes I wouldn't stress about money"; "If only I could say I'm a millionaire, people would be interested in what I have to say." If only, if only, if only!* My mindset was way off track, my perspective was twisted and my vocabulary was poor. I should have been using words and thoughts to emphasize what I *did* have and the things that were going *right;* but when you are an excuse-driven person you choose words that limit you and that do not nourish your mind.

> *"To the man who only has a hammer, everything he encounters*
> *begins to look like a nail."*
> –ABRAHAM MASLOW

I hear people using excuses every day. *"If only they would raise the minimum wage"; "If only the economy would pick up"; "If only my boss would just listen"; "If only the democrats would quit giving everything away"; "If only the republicans would stop fighting"*

If only people would quit making excuses! Right?

In fact, I actually became a more-well-rounded person because my parents didn't provide me with a silver spoon. I probably would not have done any better in college if someone else had paid for it. My grades would have been about the same, mostly B's. I learned to work hard and push from a young age and to be self-supporting, which in turn helped me get through college just fine. Using my parents as an excuse was just that, an excuse. We must appreciate the lessons within the struggles of our lives. We will always have an easy excuse to fall back on like, *"If only I made more money!"* That's a famous one many of us have used. It would go through my head over and over again. All through college, and even through my first few years of teaching, I never felt that I was making enough money and if only I just made a little more, my struggles would go away, I would be able to do all the things I wanted and I would be happier. *Wrong!* It wasn't the amount of money I was making that truly mattered; it was what I was doing with it and how I felt about it. (Remember $74.99 a month?)

As we evolve, our finances evolve. If we don't evolve our money won't grow. Today, I could still say, *"If only I made more money!"* although the truth is that I'm making 100% more now than when I first started as an educator. It has never been the money that made me happier; money was just a piece of the whole picture. Remember, we must work on all aspects of our life in order to be happy and *whole.* It is never just one thing.

If you believe that money is the key to happiness, I would like you to realize that you will never get more unless you become more. Jim Rohn, said it best, *"To earn more, you need to become more!"* This statement is so true. So, if it is money you seek to improve your life, you are on the right track by reading this book and improving yourself to become more. This brings to mind the proposed law in California where I currently live, to have the minimum wage raised statewide from $10.00 an hour to $15.00 an hour. *Why?* Did the people making $10 an hour suddenly become more valuable? Seriously? A 50% raise? Wow! Will handing them $5 more an hour help them become more? Will they start reading the books and listen to self-improvement CDs? Will they work harder? I wouldn't know since I've never been handed a 50% pay raise. In one fell swoop. But I have earned my right to a salary that's much greater than what I made when I began my professional career. I worked my way to earning more because I *became more*. I became more valuable and deserved more. I've gone to the professional improvement classes and I've read lots of books. I've listened to numerous CDs on personal growth. I've attended training sessions and paid for continued education. And I still do all these things because I'm still growing and I'm still becoming more. This process will never end. You are forever becoming either more or less. You will never reach your full potential because your full potential keeps evolving as you keep growing. This is a beautiful fact about life!

Working as a teacher for ten years, I've been to my fair share of union meetings and I've heard a lot of the complaints that *"teachers don't make enough money,"* and so on. What I do not understand in all this is why some of these people who complain don't re-channel that energy into becoming more. The excuse that their school district isn't paying them enough is not helping their life. We've already established that to earn more you must become more, so hear this, complainers: *Move up the ladder!* Go and get your master's degree or your doctorate, take some improvement classes! Read more, develop more! Yes, teachers need to be students, too. I know not all teachers complain about this and that some who do complain and don't think they are making enough have gone the route of getting higher degrees and done all the above. I suggest they either find another avenue through which they can become more valuable and hence earn more, or they look inward at their inner bully. The inner bully can easily make a $75,000 a year wage earner feel bad about it. I've been there. How do you feel about what you are currently making? How can you improve your income stream?

How do you earn more when you've reached the top of academic education or the training scale and you've continued to take the self-improvement classes, attend the seminars and read the books? You need to market yourself as someone more valuable. Hold training sessions and seminars, become the public educator to more than just your current audience. Make more sales calls. Train others wanting to better their sales. You can't expect someone else to fight your battle for a higher wage for you. Simply expecting a union to fight for a 1%, 2%, or 3% raise every year isn't making anyone more valuable. Expecting the government to raise the minimum wage isn't making anyone worthier. Complaining about life circumstances defiantly will not improve your income. We all need to become more in life!

During my eighth year of teaching, I started working more on my personal development. I was spending ten to fifteen hours every week reading and learning, reading and learning. By the end of the eighth year of my teaching career, I was making over $85,000 a year. By the end of my ninth year, I was earning over $100,000 annually. Not all that income came from my current employer. How did I do it? I went out to the marketplace and marketed myself as a more valuable person, because I was. You too can do the same, but you must work on yourself first and stop all excuses. It is up to you!

Interestingly, I started making more money in a down economy and I'm making more money today with the same company. I even make more now despite the fact that I have more responsibilities in my personal life and I'm being pulled in so many different directions. I am making more though my time is more occupied. Why? Because I am more today than I was, I am more skilled, and have become more efficient with my time. And I will continue to become more and grow with an open mind, with determination, and with an attitude that's free of excuses. I have developed this ability and so can you!

I must thank the late Jim Rohn. If it were not for the simple statement he made, which he in turn learned from his mentor, Earl Shoaff, I wouldn't be where I am today. *"To earn more, you need to become more."* That statement is so simple and yet so powerful in its truth. I hope it sticks with you. You can no longer complain to your spouse, coworkers, or your union, or the government that you are not making enough money. You just need to work on yourself to become more and you will earn more in every aspect of your life.

"Opportunity is missed by most people because it is
dressed in overalls and looks like work."
–THOMAS EDISON

Remember this excuse I used to have? *"If only I were a millionaire people would listen to me and care what I say."* That was silly to think. I talk to people every day and they listen to me. I allow my passion and purpose to drive me. Not the excuses of my past. I'm more interested now than ever before in helping others find true happiness and success. I forget the exact quote and even who said it, but it goes something like this, *"Help everyone else get what they want and you can have the world."* Well, I definitely do not want the world, but If I could leave this earth knowing that my love, passion, ideas, and wisdom has helped lead you to becoming more, to becoming happier and living a better life, my true goal will have been met. If you're only looking to be a millionaire in life, it's not going to happen. Remember your need for *purpose*? Let your desire and purpose set your sail in life. Tell yourself that if you become more, you'll be able to help more people and the more people you help, the more people will listen to you, and when more people listen to a positive message, the better things become. The better things become for the masses, the more happiness and money will naturally follow. But I will tell you loud and clear that if you allow your desire for money to come before your passion, before your purpose, you will miss out big time. Your inner bully will want you to work on getting the money first without working on you first. *Don't do it! It will not work!*

I recognize this discussion about "becoming more" has been tied up with money and the market place. I know that many of you have become more or desire to become more at your churches, in your families, and in other ways that may not directly be reflected in the form of money, but the lesson is still the same. You need to work on yourself first if you want to improve in any aspect of your *wholistic* life. You must work on you to have enhanced relationships. You must work on you to have better health. You must work on you to become more at church, at work, and at home. It all starts with you and ends with you, and any change that empowers your success will be because of you. Your quest to become more will net you so much more than just additional education or an increase in your financial worth. It will bring new experiences into your life and present you with new and valuable people to interact with and, ultimately, new and more positive ways to view yourself.

"Life is not about waiting for the storm to pass.
It's about learning how to dance in the rain"
−AUTHOR UNKNOWN

Take Control

You are In the Driver's Seat

There are two things that drive you: love, which is felt as happiness and pleasure, and fear, which sometimes translates as pain and sadness. In the above section called "Choices," we discussed the fact that everything you do is a choice. One or the other, of these two, drives your choices. You need to be mindful of which one drives your choices. Are you driven by love or fear? Happiness or sadness? Interrupt patterns that are steered by fear, pain, and sadness with new patterns driven by love, pleasure, and happiness.

"There are two basic motivating forces: fear and love. When we are afraid, we pull back from life. When we are in love, we open to all that life has to offer with passion, excitement, and acceptance. We need to learn to love ourselves first, in all our glory and our imperfections. If we cannot love ourselves, we cannot fully open to our ability to love others or our potential to create. Evolution

and all hopes for a better world rest in the fearlessness and open-hearted vision of people who embrace life."
—JOHN LENNON

Do the choices you make steer you towards happiness and away from sadness? Pain can come in many forms, be it emotional sadness, physical pain, financial pain, or fear, and generally, anything that doesn't bring you joy or positivity. Pleasure also comes in many forms. But pleasure can be tricky and can often morph into delayed pain. This delayed pain—what you do that brings you momentary pleasure but then later brings chronic pain, disease or other negative consequences—is what you need to be careful of. If you're making these negative choices and engaging in destructive habits, you may fail to realize how destructive they can be when their negative effect does not happen immediately. Think about smokers. There is often a long period between the time someone starts smoking and being ultimately diagnosed with emphysema or even lung cancer; it can take decades. Your pleasures can really be pain in disguise. You must be mindful!

Why would you choose to do something knowing sadness and pain are just around the corner? Yet you most likely engage in habits that lack long-term value. The problem with making decisions that feel good for the moment, but lack long-term benefits, is that your brain has been falsely programmed to associate these choices, these habits with pleasure. *You're tricking yourself!* If on the other hand, you can immediately start associating a negative habit with pain, you will be more readily driven to stop it. You must remind yourself of the downfall that comes with the negative habit before you engage in it. You have to alert yourself that this is a cycle of pain.

Let's look at the example of somebody who continuously overeats. As they are eating, they're finding pleasure in the act of eating. But it causes them pain later as they realized they've gained weight and experience an overall decline in health and lower self-esteem. Overeating can be triggered by many things; an overeater may associate eating healthfully with feeling deprived, or an authoritarian parent, or with feelings of comfort. Either way, the associations they have with overeating are detrimental and negative to their welfare. They have allowed themselves to overeat because they've told themselves that overeating unhealthy food brings pleasure, brings them a sense of comfort. They have tied the association of pleasure with overeating. The pleasure is only momentary and so it creates a destructive cycle that keeps them coming back for more bouts of overeating. *Why?* Because the brain craves that fix of pleasure, pleasure, pleasure, just like any other addictions.

You must identify the pain before you begin to overeat or before you do anything that brings the delayed pain cycle on. First, you have to start changing your mindset and get real. Begin to associate the true negative impact that the action has on your life. Think about what you feel while, you overeat, what you feel immediately after, and what you feel within the hours and days to come. You must repeat the negative consequences that will follow and, repeat them over and over and over again in your mind. On the flip side, you need to simultaneously give yourself the okay to eat something you want without adding the feeling of guilt. For example, if you find yourself binge eating you must first identify the trigger. What brought on this specific bout of overeating? Was the trigger a text message? Exposure to a TV show? Was the trigger a sudden feeling of being out of control due to a call from a creditor or dropping your kids off at your ex-spouse's home? Once you can consciously identify the immediate cause of your desire to overeat at that time, you need to remind yourself of the domino effect that will take place after the binge, going through exactly what that domino effect will be as specifically as possible. Finally, you need to set up a controlled binge environment. Yes, I'm saying if you know you're an overeater, you must at least take control of the situation. How do you do that? Well, let's say you binge on chips or cookies. Before you dive into the packages and potentially finish the entire bag, set up a controlled display. Get out a nice plate and set three to five cookies or one handful of chips on the plate, *then put the package away!* Now allow yourself eat everything on the plate *guilt-free.* Tell yourself you will be completely satisfied when you finish what is on that plate. Tell yourself that it's completely okay that you ate this because you are in control. It will nourish your body and you have a *measured amount* so that you are eating less than you normally would. You know that eating 3-5 cookies is not healthy, but isn't it better than eating an entire package of cookies? In your moments of being "out-of-control," *get control by controlling your thoughts!* Over time, these little victories will stop you from eating even the 3-5 cookies, and satisfying you with perhaps, only one. In this way, you won't collide with guilt when you're done, which might often drive you to eat even more.

Remember, whenever you binge, think first about the trigger, then the collateral damage in the domino effect, then set up a controlled setting with a measured amount and allow yourself to enjoy that amount guilt free. Remember that as you repeat these "binges" you should be decreasing the measured amount. You will become mindful of what's happening in the moment. You are also allowing your better self to control the situation, not your inner bully. *You* are in the driver's seat.

Here's another example of how you are driven by pain and pleasure. Do you exercise regularly? If you do, you know there are days that you may wake up not feeling all that great, but you know you need to workout, so you pull yourself out of bed and head to the gym. *Why?* Because you associate this tired feeling as being only temporary and you associate your main goal of exercising with improved health and good feelings throughout the day. You associate a morning exercise routine with positive feelings. On the flip side, if you are the person who avoids physical exercise, you may associate exercise with negative thoughts, like pain and soreness. With this negative association, you will never enjoy exercising. You will not keep up a regular exercise routine if you do not change your mindset. You need to get into the driver's seat and steer your health. You must rethink exercise and your associations with it. You should start by thinking of how great you'll feel when you're done, how wonderful your clothes will fit and how energized you'll be in the weeks to come.

If there's something you want to change in your life, you must change your mindset. A good way to start is by reprogramming your brain to either attach pleasure, happiness, love, or pain, fear, or sadness as appropriate to the behavior you want to change. So, if you're the overeater you'll need to associate overeating with pain over and over and over again in your head. If you don't like to exercise, you need to associate how much joy and how great working out will make you feel. There's that saying, *"You are what you eat."* It should be, *"You are what you think."*

Let's take one more example, the concept of depression. If you think you're depressed and you continuously say you're depressed and your work life sucks and you have no friends, guess what? You will always dislike work, feel like you have no friends, and feel depressed when you show up to work. You will continually push people away from yourself and you will always think your life sucks and always feel depressed! I went through a struggle like this for a very long time, always thinking I was depressed, even going to the doctor to get prescriptions that I thought would help me, when what I really needed was to change my mindset. I needed to reprogram my brain to think, *I am a happy person,* not a depressed one. I needed to say, *my job is great and I am thankful I get to go to work every day.* I needed to remind myself of how wonderful life is and that things will only get better!

I know this seems really simple; it *is* really simple. The challenging part is that it takes time and repetitive self-talk to shift your thinking and reprogram your mindset. It's just like exercising. Your brain is a muscle and you have to continuously exercise your brain until it associates pain and pleasure properly. Be mindful and note what thoughts and practices you have that trigger unhealthy habits and healthy habits. Take control of your habits by taking control of what you associate those habits with. Redirect your thoughts and actions to benefit you, the driver.

Take a moment and list 3 things that you choose to do because they bring you pleasure:

1.

2.

3.

Will each of these bring you pleasure 1, 2, 3, 10 and 20 years from today? Are these three things moving you forward towards your goals? Do these things help fulfill your purpose?

List three choices you habitually make that you know are not moving you forward:

1.

2.

3.

You need to continuously associate these three things above with the worst-case scenario. How will these things beat you down in the long haul and make you carry extra weight and burdens in your life? (Maybe they already have.) Whatever your three negative habits are, you need to play them out in detail through their last negative domino effects and take a stand. Tell yourself, *"I don't want this! This is not going to happen! I am strong and I am in the driver's seat. I am in control."* Then substitute that old, outgrown, bad choice, the disease-driven habit, with something that will bring you happiness and pleasure, something that enhances your dreams and goals. Visualize removing the old choice, throwing it away, and inserting in its place, a new, positive, pleasurable choice. I must say this again: visualize yourself removing the old choice, throwing it away, and inserting a new positive pleasurable choice in its place. As you do this, visualize yourself smiling and in the driver's seat of your life. *You are in control!*

> *"Look closely at the present you are constructing:*
> *it should look like the future you are dreaming."*
> –ALICE WALKER

Focus, Learn, and Move Forward

"Where focus goes, energy flows." For the longest time I would do as many projects at one time that I could fit in my schedule. If the saying has any truth to it, my focus of trying to do multiple projects naturally limited the amount of energy I could put towards any single project and consequently, I was using only a fraction of my energy on any one. I realized this was hurting my personal and professional life and I needed to focus on no more than one or two projects at a time. As I was a, *"Yes"* person this also meant that I could not say *yes* to everything.

"Multitasking" is sometimes viewed as a positive skill, but I don't believe it is. Multitasking creates a lot of extra stress in our lives. There is already enough chaos in the world around us. The ability to have a healthy focus on something is key. People like to boast that they multitask. I used to say the same thing. But on my journey, I've learned to limit the extra noise I create by not trying to do everything myself or doing things all at once. With this I have become more focused. You, too, can learn to have new habits through *focusing*.

Have you ever had someone talk to you while your mind was somewhere else so that you had no idea what was just said? Maybe you had some general idea regarding what it was about, but you missed the details because of all the noise in your mind. It's happened to me. It's what happens when your mind tries to focus on too many things at once and starts doing somersaults. Maybe while your child performed at an event, you were returning emails from your phone, or daydreaming about something else you needed to do, then realized that everyone was applauding for something that your child had done. Everyone looked at you with excitement to see your reaction, but you completely missed what had happened! Maybe you pretended that you knew what had happened and you smiled but you really missed it. I've missed things my kids did. When you try and do too much your energy cracks and you end up with a crippled focus on everything you're trying to do. Your mind will pull you in different directions and you miss things. Staying focused can be difficult; don't make it harder by spreading your attention too thin.

When your mind goes from A to B, your mind is on B leaving A, abandoned yet taking some of your mental energy. You may mistake going back and forth, back and forth, between A and B with multitasking but are you really doing two things at once? No. You stop A when you go to B and then get back, eventually, to A. This becomes problematic if you're trying to do more than two things within a short period of time. Your "multitasking" is really you, going from one thing (A) to the next (B) to the next (C). In doing so, you disburse some energy with each, in turn being left with less energy for them all. It's a tiring process, emotionally draining, and not as productive as if you were to just focus on one thing. Remember, once that one thing is completed, you can move on to the next task with all your energy. You can cross it off your mental "to do" list, which affords you energy and mental focus for your next task, as you move on. The more simultaneous tasks you have, the more you have to worry about and the more inner stress you create.

Let me show you what attempting to do five different things at once would look like in a visual. Assume you have five children (I am sure this possibility may already scare some of you, ha-ha). Each child is in a different room and you are helping each get dressed for the day. Your goal to have five kids ready in the shortest time with the least amount of added stress. You start in the first room and get Child #1's shirt on, then you head to the second room to help Child #2 with her shirt, and so on. By the time, you get to Child #5, the other four children are running around in their rooms and some may even have taken their shirt off. You're feeling stressed and frustrated but you have to keep on going. You go back to help those children put their shirt back on and then help Child #1 put his pants on and then go to Child #2 to put on her skirt and so on until you work your way to Child #5 in the last room. You're coming and going, coming and going. You have created a lot of mental stress and chaos. You're feeling anxious and the kids are feeling anxious as well. You are worrying about Child #1, Child #2, Child #3, Child #4 and Child #5. Once done with shirts, pants and skirts, you now go back to Child #1 to help with socks then to Child #2 and so on. Unfortunately, kids do not keep their socks on very long when their shoes are not on and you can't be in five places at once, so off their socks go and you will have to do the same task over gain.

You are back to Child #1. This time, you put on his socks and his shoes. Child #1 is ready! You take Child #1 with you to Child #2. You help Child #2 put socks and shoes on and take both children with you to Child #3. At this point you're feeling much better because you're feeling a sense of accomplishment and control. Why? Because you have completed two of the five projects, but most importantly, you are not worried about the first two unattended anymore and your focus is narrowed down to the last three. Finally, you have all five children ready to go. All five projects are completed. You finish with a high level of stress, but also with a sense of accomplishment.

How could this have been done more efficiently and with less stress? By helping one child at a time. Get Child #1 dressed completely from head to toe. This way, you wouldn't have had to worry about this child (or project) becoming undone because you were there and focused on it from start to finish without having to worry about the other children (or projects), knowing they were there waiting without destroying anything you had started. And, when you finish with Child #1 (Project #1), you no longer need to be concerned with that child (project). You move on to Child #2, completely dress that child and move on like this through to Child #5.

When you try to do multiple things at once, you take on additional stress and worry, that you carry around with you, because as you move on to the next thing, what you leave behind isn't finished yet and therefore saps some of your energy and mental clarity and allows room for unknown factors to come in and mess up what you have accomplished. On the other hand, when you stick with one thing from start to finish, you stress less, worry less and don't exhaust yourself. Try approaching things you need to accomplish, one at a time, from start to finish and see how you feel.

> *"Our greatest weapon against stress is our ability to choose one thought over another."*
> –WILLIAM JAMES

You may find yourself creating unnecessary stress at work. If you are anything like me, your wandering mind and lack of focus can impact your work life. Remember, everything is connected. With a deadline approaching for my very important newsletter, I was creating unimportant emails. When I was supposed to be making a phone call, I'd be wandering onto different websites and watching videos on YouTube (albeit videos on personal development). This lack of focus was a problem. When I allowed this sort of thing to happen, I felt out of control—because I was out of control. Why was I allowing the day to control me? Why wasn't I controlling my day? Do you ever feel like this?

This potential for a lack of focus, has grown exponentially with technology. There's your work email, your personal email, Facebook, Twitter, Snapchat, Instagram, and so on. Trying to stay focused on any one task is challenging enough but add the virtual world to this madness along with our fast-paced lives and it can make you want to pull your hair out. Unfortunately, it doesn't stop there. In the changing roles of men and women in the new era, life becomes even more complicated. No longer is it the role of the female to stay at home, focus on the kids, and keep a tidy home. Nor is the man able to just focus on work then come home to throw his feet up and relax after a long day. Today, both women and men have dual roles, giving them more to focus on. More often than not, both sexes work full time, take care of the kids, and take part in housework. Everyone is going in different directions and it can become chaotic, so we might hire housekeepers, gardeners, nannies, tutors, and others to help get the job done. You do not have the luxury of fulfilling only one of these roles; you must work to juggle all the various aspects of your life. *But how?*

I believe a primary reason for one's lack of focus is due to the emotional burden that comes from trying to do it all. Your focus is grabbed from external things in your environment as well as from the emotional factors in your life. Have you ever felt too overwhelmed by one thing to finish something else that needed your focus? You've hit on another reason to check your inner bully. The noise your inner bully creates in your mind robs you of much-needed energy to focus.

If you feel this section on focus is all over the place it's because this is the reality many of you are living. You are spread too thin in today's world.

The demands society makes on you combined with the demands you make on yourself will break you down if you are burning the candle at both ends. So how do you focus? How much should you focus on? What do you focus on?

Remember, where your focus goes, energy flows. *What is your goal? What do you want?* I encourage you to make a list. You should list your higher priorities at the top and lower ones at the bottom. Once you've listed what you're sure are your top priorities, prioritize them on your timeline if appropriate. For example, if you have five things you feel are high priorities you may need to get them done in some order. If you have one major project you are working on, though it may not need to be completed for several weeks, be sure to set aside specific times every day to complete a part of it—a task within the task. Be sure this time is only dedicated to this project (no wandering mind and no other tasks around to distract you). Every time you work on it, you can cross that project off your daily list and move on to the next priority. Crossing this task off your list every day that you work on it—even before it is 100% done—allows your mind to release it. You've completed the part of the task as you had set out to do and now you can move on. Remember, you've already planned every task out so as long as you stick to the plan you'll be done by your deadline and there is no need to add emotional stress by worrying. This is exactly why you're going to plan out your priorities and write them down.

Use Extreme Focus. Extreme focus prevents you from drifting off. It's like shooting a free throw in basketball. You step up to the line with a plan. There are things you must do before the ball leaves your hands: First, you set your feet. Then you get your hands in position on the ball. Maybe you dribble the ball at the line 2-3 times and then look at the hoop. You focus on the front of the rim, keeping your elbow in, you bend your knees, and only then do you take the shot. That plan was made before you stepped up to the line. Your mental checklist: position, hands, dribble, eyes up-elbow in, knees bent, and shoot! You've made the shot a thousand times before but you have to focus to make it again, because if your mind wanders, if you lose one degree of focus, if you don't keep everything in line to make that shot, it's all worth nothing; you will miss the basket. This is true even if you've made the same shot thousands of times before. You need extreme focus. Not a single person can challenge your focus when you step up to that line. You know what your goal is and you know what action steps you must take within a certain time frame if you are to be successful. You know to quiet the unnecessary noise in your mind.

> *"Good, better, best. Never let it rest. Till your good is better and*
> *your better is best."*
> –ST. JEROME

Don't go through life on autopilot or you'll miss all the good stuff that focusing will bring you. Focus brings a sense of accomplishment and success. But like exercising a muscle, you need to exercise your ability to focus on different things over time to continue showing improvement.

You can't just keep doing squats with ten-pound weights to show progress, you need to change it up. You may have to add weight or do more repetitions to keep challenging yourself. The same is true with focus. When you're doing something and your mind starts to go on autopilot you need to change what you're doing or how you're doing it. Remember: Focusing should actually provide you with energy. If focusing on something doesn't energize you, it's a sign that you are probably trying to focus on too many things at once.

If you have ever learned a new skill you probably know, there's a learning curve. Focusing on a task and making that task become automatic takes time, but I am sure you feel energized with each improvement you make. The goal of learning any skill is to master that skill until it becomes automatic. Once your new skill becomes as automatic as a habit, you can push yourself even more, both personally and professionally by developing new things to focus on.

Mastery of a skill only comes as a result of focusing on one step and then the next. It's like learning to dribble a basketball: first you learn to dribble with your dominant hand and then with your non-dominant hand. Then you become capable of dribbling while running down the court. Finally, you learn to dribble and then either shoot or pass the ball. It all started with extreme focus on how to dribble the ball up and down, up and down with your dominant hand. Your game improved step-by-step. It was only after you focused on the first basic skill of dribbling until you'd mastered it, that you could move on to the next progression.

Focusing is great for the body and the mind. Just think how boring it would be if every time you picked up a basketball you just stood there dribbling it with your right hand, up and down, up and down. You would get bored very quickly. Don't do that with your mind, your body, or your life. Learn how to run and dribble. Learn how to shoot the ball. Learn new tricks and the result may be that you score your first three-pointer.

Extreme Focus will get you far in life. Your focus can only be as strong as your detailed plan (vision) with deadline dates (goals). You must take action to get your project started. The best way to start moving forward is by putting your top priorities down on paper, visualize what you want to achieve, and then take action to make it happen, one priority at a time. You must have some tools in our toolkit to help you with your focus. Here are some things you can do to improve your focus:

#1: Put your phone away! This is the very first key to obtaining Extreme Focus. Turn it *off*! I've been to so many meetings where people will set their phone down on the conference table. (Yes, even when you put it on silent, your phone lights up with every message, which is distracting and takes your mind away from what you should be focusing on). You need to stop using your phone as a pacifier. Our phones provide us adults with comfort and they are addictive. Yes addictive! Do you get irritated when you misplace your phone, or when the battery is dying, or if you forgot it at home? All of these steal your focus. I know we all accomplish a lot of work with our phones, but we also lose a lot of focus because of them. Try going phoneless for a day and see what happens. Are you more productive? Are you aggravated? Do you have more peace of mind?

#2: Write down your tasks! When you have a bunch of tasks that you need to complete, write them all down and then prioritize them. Have you ever started organizing your house and planned to start with your closet (which I think is the hardest thing to do) then find yourself cleaning the bathroom? Or maybe, you realize that you started five different things and never really finished any of them? If you're like my husband, you'll start cleaning the garage and find yourself working instead, on your dirt bike or washing the car. What happened to cleaning the garage? This happens to all of us.

#3: Have a game plan! You have to map out your plan and follow it step-by-step. Have a written game plan! Writing down the "how-tos," the steps needed to fulfill the task, will help keep you focused and efficient. When you know what you are doing and you're focused on the task, you will complete it faster and complete it with more mindfulness. However, when you're not focused, there are too many options that make you less efficient. Focus with a written game plan to know the direction you are going and you'll save time, be more efficient, and distractions will be limited.

If you follow the above rules for obtaining extreme focus, your focus will make you far more efficient and allow you to be energized throughout each task. Remember, when you're focused, you can accomplish a lot more in less time because you have more energy. When you're focused, the work to be done in a ten-hour day could be done in seven hours because you're able to get everything done more efficiently without distraction. *Don't procrastinate! Don't multitask!* Get a plan and focus on one task, get it done, and move on to the next.

Remember that focus is a skill you learn and, like all skills, needs to be practiced. You need to work on focus every day of your life. If you don't, things will become overwhelming and you will become frustrated, even stagnant; you will not progress to the next skill or next level. Make yourself pay attention and focus on where you're at, what you're doing, and on developing more skills. Practice, practice, practice, and *stay focused!*

"You will never reach your destination if you stop
and throw stones at every dog that barks."
–WINSTON CHURCHILL

Losing vs. Failing

You know the saying, "You don't learn to win by always winning." Nowadays, it seems everybody is a winner; everybody gets a trophy. I think we have confused *losing* with *failure*. To lose is not to fail; yet we use the words interchangeably.

As a parent, you don't want to see your kid struggle or be so challenged that he or she gets frustrated; however, losing is an important part of life. You need to be challenged and your children need to be challenged. You need to lose, so you can learn how to win. The only time you fail is when you learn nothing from a loss because you ignore the lesson to be learned. You shouldn't confuse losing with failure but rather, program yourself to believe that there is no losing; there are only outcomes that we must learn from.

When you associate losing as a failure, you begin to set lower goals for yourself; after all, no one likes to lose. You mustn't hold back. You don't have to be okay with being "average." We've already agreed that when you set goals higher then you truly believe you can achieve, you will ultimately end up accomplishing more. If you don't reach those higher goals, don't tell yourself you've failed and revert back to your insecurities and lower your standards. Instead, grasp the lesson to be learned. This is where you need to change your thinking. To come up short or to lose is not a failure; learn from it.

"Problems are not stop signs, they are guidelines."
–ROBERT H. SCHULLER

You have way more to give than you think. *We all do!* You are capable of achieving so much more success then you believe. You always overestimate how successful and smart others are and underestimate how successful and smart you are becoming.

Think of 3 big goals that you want to achieve. Write them down.

1.

2.

3.

Now, make each of those three goals ten times more ambitious

1.

2.

3.

Remember, it is better to set higher goals and come up a little short then to set your goals lower and end up with less. If you come up short on your major goals, you haven't failed! You've simply had an outcome and an opportunity to learn and grow.

History has shown us over and over again the importance of **attitude**. Continuing to try, setting high goals, and learning from your experiences are of paramount importance. I assure you that any successful person will tell you they wish they'd set their goals even higher from the start. I'm certain they will also tell you that they've learned a great deal from the mistakes they've made along their journey and that they needed those mistakes and losses in their past to get them to their current success. I know I needed all the mistakes of my past to get me to my present success. There is no way I could be where I am today if my life had always been a win and all had been smooth sailing.

Take some time this week to find two or three people you know to be very successful. Maybe they're financially successful, or perhaps they're a great parent, or believer; talk to them and ask them how they have become so successful and how have they accomplished the goals you admire. Ask them how they've gotten to where they are. What mistakes had they made? What were their goals when they first started their journey? Ask them what lessons they've learned along the way.

"I have not failed. I've just found 10,000 ways that won't work."
–THOMAS A. EDISON

Surround Yourself with Success

You must give yourself a fighting chance for true success. Throughout this book, we've been discussing what you need to do to achieve more success. You know you need to live a *wholistic* lifestyle, make better choices, take care of yourself, be more mindful of your life, stop being reductionist, reprogram your brain, focus, and juggle it all. You also need to reach up and surround yourself with high achievers, people that have been more successful than you have been so far, people who are more connected than you are. It is important to be aware of what successful traits look like and what success acts like. You should strive to develop those traits within yourself. You need to do what successful people do and commit, commit, commit.

Some people think they need to figure everything out before they take action. They feel they need to plan and analyze every detail before taking the first step. This is a paralyzing way to think. I challenge you to commit first, make a plan then start taking action, and figure it out as you move along, just as you have done in this book. The problem with trying to figure every little detail out beforehand is that you can't! Have you ever planned for something big, some big event or some big challenge only to realize you've had to adapt, overcome, and improvise a great deal when an unforeseen thing unfolded? Or despite all your planning, something you hadn't planned for ultimately throws you off? A planned wedding is a good example if this. You've no doubt heard the nightmare stories of the bride who worries about every little detail, every single moment up until the "big day," and thinks she's fully prepared for everything and then *boom*! Something goes wrong and it hits her like a ton to bricks. It hits her so hard she's in the bathroom crying at her own wedding!

How can this be? Hadn't she planned for everything? She added so much stress to herself by trying to over analyze everything, so when something she hadn't planned for happened, she was paralyzed with disbelief and the added weight of the day brought her to tears. This should never happen.

Contrast that example with the scenario at my wedding. I knew I didn't want to be that bride. I didn't plan out every detail. I booked a venue, gave my mom and best friend a budget and said, "I would like to be married in six weeks. Here's the venue, budget, and the date." I knew my mom would be great at organizing because she is a good organizer and I knew my best friend would be good at planning a beautiful event because she had been to many weddings. (She also witnessed the traumatized bride and she knew I didn't want to be one.) I trusted she would help make my day run smoothly. So, what happened? I got married and had a great time at my wedding! Did anything go wrong? Maybe, I honestly don't know! I mean, who gets through any day without something going wrong? But if there was a problem, it didn't stress me out in the least. It helped that I surrounded myself with successful people who could plan and execute a successful event and that I didn't try to plan every detailed second of the day before it happened.

Surround yourself with people who are successful in whatever you are doing and don't try to analyze or predict every little thing, for if you do, you'll be greatly disappointed when something doesn't go the way you thought it would. Remember: Analysis can equal paralysis. When you think of every miniscule detailed part of a successful event or achievement it becomes overwhelming. That's why you need to simply take action and start doing before you get caught in the paralysis of analysis. When all's said, and done, you can't plan every little detail or prepare for every contingency that might get in the way of your success but it is paramount that you get people around you that blossom within the event or area you are committing too.

It's good to be prepared. It's good to have 20/20 foresight. But I encourage you to stay away from trying to prepare every little detail. You can worry about the details once you have begun taking massive action. Once you start achieving that success, you can look at the details and see how to become even more successful. You can look to others and ask how you can do better, but you have to get started first or there will be no success story to tell. Take action to move forward, or be in a standstill. Don't get derailed with the details!

"If you hang out with chickens, you're going to cluck and if you hang out with eagles, you're going to fly."
–STEVE MARABOLI

Nourish Your Senses

All too often you neglect or take for granted your own body's senses. I think we all do! God has blessed you with triumphant ways to communicate with yourself and the world around you. There are the illuminating sights we see, the harmony of songs we hear, the invigorating tastes and smells of life, along with the softness of touch. You derive infinite pleasures from the combination of all your senses working collectively. It is of prime importance that you nourish your sense of sight, smell, hearing, touch, and taste in positive ways. Though your mind is not a sense, it interprets everything that your senses perceive and embodies your thoughts.

Every day, you are bombarded with thousands of images. You don't have a lot of control over some of those images, as for example, the traffic you see on the highway, the bad accident you pass, and the people you see on the streets and the people you see at work. But you do have control over the images you see on your computer screen and the images you choose to watch on TV. You also have control over the images you see when you choose to participate in an activity. You can choose to see the sun come up on a hike. You can choose to support a loved one when you watch them take part in a sporting event or a music recital. The majority of what we see is what we choose to surround ourselves with. If you choose to watch negative TV shows that are constantly depicting murder and drama, you are not nurturing your vision. In turn, this is not good for your soul.

You also hear many different noises and messages throughout every day. The things you have control over when it comes to your hearing is, in part, comprised of the music and messages you listen to in the car. You can choose to listen to upbeat positive music or you can choose to listen to negative music. You can choose to listen to a positive, inspiring message or you can choose to listen to negative talk radio or a talk show where individuals are picked apart. You can choose to listen to your children when they talk to you and tell you a story about their day or you can choose to ignore them while your attention is drawn to your phone.

Just as you nourish your vision and your hearing, you must also nourish your sense of touch. You can choose to hug your kids every morning. You can choose to hug and kiss your spouse or loved one when leaving for the day or you can yell, *"I'm leaving,"* and head out the door for the day. You can choose to hold hands with a loved one or stay disconnected. You can choose to see and touch a pretty flower and smell the fragrance of its whole bloom or you can walk right by it without a glance. You can choose to pat someone on the back or give them a high five, just because you are happy to see them or you can just grin and say, *"Hi."* You can choose to feel for a hard-crisp apple in the produce section and pick up healthy food that will enhance your taste buds, or you can throw a bag of chips in your grocery cart. You can choose to walk with bare feet on the grass, sand, or along the ocean or you can choose to wear synthetic soles and miss out on the opportunity to connect to the earth. The choice is up to you!

It is vital that you use all your senses and nourish each sense in enhancing, positive, energizing ways. This section can be connected with the earlier life lesson shared in the beginning: *you are surrounded by what you want, and you are what you surround yourself with.* When you strive to nourish and use all your senses in complete ways, you enhance your whole life.

Below, list some everyday patterns that you take part in that impact your sense of:

Touch:

Taste:

Sight:

Hearing:

Smell:

Lastly, how are you enhancing your sixth sense, namely, your mind that impacts your thoughts? This book is a great start to nourishing that sixth sense!

> *"Keep your face always toward the sunshine—*
> *and shadows will fall behind you."*
> –WALT WHITMAN

Keep Evolving

It is my hope that you begin to approach your life from a *wholistic* standpoint and begin to make decisions based on your *whole* self, and on your *whole* environment. You must believe it is possible to work on all aspects of your life simultaneously. Recall that it is not necessary to balance them all equally or that the amount of effort need be equal in all areas; you only need to stay in touch with every aspect of your life and put some amount of effort into them all.

Remember there is no magic bullet, or miracle pill. It is never just one thing. *Wholism* is the key to unlocking your full potential. It is what has completely freed me from my dark days of depression and my days of feeling "less than." It has given me freedom from my own paralyzing thoughts; it's that important. You need to approach your life in a *wholistic* way. You must be *whole* to be *happy* and it is up to *you* to practice wholeness.

It is time to ask yourself some more questions:

1. Do you acknowledge that any one aspect of your life can weigh down other aspects of your life?

2. Are you being *wholistic* in your life? In other words, are you working on all aspects of your life *every day*? Use this checklist below to ask yourself which aspects of your life you are addressing and which areas are you neglecting.

- You're Health?

  - ❖ Spiritual Health?

  - ❖ Physical Health?

  - ❖ Nutritional Health?

  - ❖ Emotional Health?

  - ❖ Relationship Health?

    - ▪ Family Relationships?

    - ▪ Friend Relationships?

    - ▪ Coworker Relationships?

    - ▪ Stranger Relationships?

  - ❖ Financial Health?

    - ▪ Financial Education?

    - ▪ Planning your Finances?

      - ☐ Spending Wisely?

☐ Saving your Money?

☐ Growing your Money?

❖ Pursuing Hobbies and Personal Development?

▪ Do you do something every day that you enjoy?

▪ Do you do something you personally enjoy, just for you?

▪ Do you do something every day with your family that you all enjoy?

❖ Are you learning something new?

▪ Something that makes you smile?

▪ Something that challenges your focus?

▪ Do you read or listen to something every day that inspires you?

All of these aspects are important. The worksheets in this book have been designed to assist you in keeping a close look on your progress in living *wholistically,* every day. To keep your inner bully at bay and live a *wholistic* life, you must strive to address each area above daily. If you find yourself struggling with this connect with me and use the tools provided at **www. HapyWholeYou.com**, this takes time! Also, if you want a quick tune-up download the eBook "Beat Your Inner Bully in 14-Days." Available on the HappyWholeYou.com website.

"Our greatest journey is our internal voyage.
Take time to discover yourself.
Find your essence, the unique you.
Advertisers want to classify you.
You are an individual.
Live your own life."
–PATRICK LINDSAY

Worksheet #6—"Add-In Method" 52-Week Challenge

To live *wholistically* is to address all the areas of your life. I have created a 52-week Challenge that you will use as a tool for improving your life. You'll be using this worksheet for the entire year! It is very simple to use and will help you include 52 new practices into your life over the next 365 days. It is not directed to any one specific diet or workout plan, but a strategic way to approach improving your *whole* self, using the Add-In Method. Simply add one new and positive thing into your life every week. At the end of the year you will have added 52 new positive practices to your life!

For example:

Week 1: Write: Every morning I will drink 16 oz. of water upon rising. I will do this every day.

Week 2: Write: Every mid-morning I will eat one small apple. You will do this every day, along with, drinking your 16 oz. of water.

Week 3: Write: Every night I will write down one thing I am proud of that I accomplished that day. You will do this every day, along with drinking 16 oz. of water every morning, and eating a mid-morning apple.

Week 4: Write: Every day I will take a minimum of 10,000 steps. (If you already get 10,000 steps a day, increase your current average number of steps by 3,000. Are you wondering when you will have the time to do this? Add a walk during your break times—even a 5-10-minute walk counts. Park your car in the parking space furthest from your destination wherever you go. Find ways to increase your steps within your daily routine.) You will do this every day, along with drinking 16 oz. of water, eating your mid-morning apple, and writing down your daily proud moment.

Week 5: Write: Every day I will stand up, smile, reach for the sky, and then touch my toes. I will keep that smile on for 30 seconds! You will do this every day, along with, drinking 16 oz. of water, eating your mid-morning apple, writing down one thing every night that you're proud of, and walking 10,000+ steps a day.

Week 6: Write: Every morning I will take 30 seconds to hug my spouse, my children, and anyone else that lives under the same roof as me. You will do this every day, along with, your first 5 weeks of challenges.

YEARLY ADD-IN CALENDAR

Start Date   End Date

Week 1	Week 27
Week 2	Week 28
Week 3	Week 29
Week 4	Week 30
Week 5	Week 31
Week 6	Week 32
Week 7	Week 33
Week 8	Week 34
Week 9	Week 35
Week 10	Week 36
Week 11	Week 37
Week 12	Week 38
Week 13	Week 39
Week 14	Week 40
Week 15	Week 41
Week 16	Week 42
Week 17	Week 43
Week 18	Week 44
Week 19	Week 45
Week 20	Week 46
Week 21	Week 47
Week 22	Week 48
Week 23	Week 49
Week 24	Week 50
Week 25	Week 51
Week 26	Week 52

happywholeyou.com

www.HappyWholeYou.com

The Beginning

The Final Piece

Thank you for taking this journey with me. Please remember that to be truly happy and *whole* you must recognize that every aspect of your life is important, for every aspect influences the others. Every single choice that you make influences your next choice and by that one choice, you are choosing many things. By choosing *wholism,* you are choosing to silence your inner bully!

You must have a healthy mind. You must have a healthy heart. You must have a healthy body. You must have healthy relationships. You must have a healthy work life. All of these go hand in hand. You will not have one without the other. You may be doing better in some areas than others, but it's important to always keep improving your weaker areas and that in turn, will help improve your overall strength.

Your life is what you make of it. Your life is happening now and it is happening exactly how you want your life to happen. You are where you are in life because of every single decision you've made up to this very point. It is the result of how you've chosen to react to different events, how you've chosen to take care of yourself and how you've chosen to take care of everything around you. You have created all of this. You have everything you need within you to grow into the person you want to be. You have everything you need in you to serve your purpose.

How do you want your life to change?

What words will you use to rewrite your song?

How does the beat of your new song feel to your soul?

> *"Once you replace negative thoughts with positive ones, you'll start to have positive results!"*
> –WILLIE NELSON

Happy. Whole. You.

You did it! You have gone through all the chapters in this book, and have answered many questions. I hope you have uncovered negative patterns in your life that you are now eager to shed. You now have few more tools for your toolbox and I will keep providing you with more. All the worksheets I designed are here to help you continue on your journey of becoming a more *happy-whole-you*. Many of these worksheets can be downloaded from the Happy-Whole-You site. You also have access to recent and past blog articles and can sign up for the free Happy-Whole-You newsletter.

It is with an open heart I have shared my journey with you. I hope you feel a sense of connection with me and more importantly a deeper connection within yourself. You are AMAZING! You deserve happiness and wholeness. Press on my friend and enjoy all the missteps along the way, as they will strengthen you!

Join me on Facebook, Instagram, and Twitter @HappyWholeYou and on Snap Chat @Vanna2go.

About the Author

Anna Marie is a ball of fire. Her ability to capture an audience at one of her seminars is moving. She is relatable, a true teacher and a leader. Her mission to bring true happiness and success to others never stops. She has dedicated her whole life to empowering others through health and wellness practices. She was not always the upbeat successful person she is today. She went through many struggles just like the next person, however, she has discovered and created a "wholistic" approach to life and repeats an anthem that has teens, stay-at-home moms, and

successful businesswomen saying, "Stop Bullying Yourself!" The moment you tell yourself this phrase is the moment you empower yourself to move forward towards your goals and dreams. Anna Marie brings hope and motivation to those who have given up on their ultimate desires.

Anna Marie grew up in Charlotte, Michigan a small town outside of Lansing, Michigan. She attended Western Michigan University and then moved out west to begin her career. She is a successful business owner, writer, speaker, and the wellness specialist for the largest high school district in the state of California. She spent a decade as a classroom teacher and over sixteen years as a fitness coach. She has also been featured on air with an NBC affiliate as a health a wellness expert. Her work has been published in local publications and she has also spent three years working with an INC top 100 company leading over 250 team members. Anna Marie loves business, health, and helping others. She is the founder of the Happy-Whole-You coaching programs and wellness centers. She enjoys working with school districts, businesses and individuals to better their lives and communities. She is an avid runner and loves to rollerblade. Anna Marie currently lives in California with her husband and two children, Louis and Garity.

To contact Anna Marie for speaking engagements, trainings, coaching needs or consulting please e-mail her at AnnaMarie@HappyWholeYou.com.

Morgan James
Speakers Group

We connect Morgan James published authors with live and online events and audiences who will benefit from their expertise.

Morgan James makes all of our titles available
through the Library for All Charity Organization.

www.LibraryForAll.org